KU-331-464

REMY MARTIN
83

6 of the best: Tait's Top Horses

Olympic gold medallist & world champion BLYTH TAIT
with KATE GREEN

David & Charles

56

contents

how it all BEGAN

My earliest memory of riding is when I was ten. My first pony was a little grey Welsh Mountain mare called Flash, who was the ideal beginner's pony. One day when I was trying to get her to jump over a row of upturned buckets she refused point blank to have anything to do with it. I was getting extremely frustrated and my mother, who knows nothing about riding, was kindly giving instructions from the window. Eventually she suggested that I should come in for some lunch and try again later, so I tied Flash up and stalked up to the house in a real temper. When I came out after lunch to have another go at jumping the buckets, I discovered Flash had had a foal!

I was brought up in Whangarei, which is north of Auckland, and right from those early days my parents Bob and Glenise have always been very supportive of my riding career. I have two older sisters, Karen and Sandi, neither of whom are horsey. Sandy now runs a computer company with her husband and Karen is married to a policeman.

My father has been particularly influential. His profession is real estate, but horses have been

above *Participating in one of New Zealand's now traditional sports!*

right *My parents, Bob and Glenise, who have always been very supportive at the World Games at The Hague*

a long-time hobby. He always managed to choose me the right sort of ponies so that I was never over-mounted, which was instrumental in my remaining keen. I was never frightened and grew up with total confidence in ponies. I didn't have flashy ponies, but they were always clever and safe, especially my best one, Mandara, whom I rode at the Pony Club Championships.

My father has Thoroughbred brood mares and prepares horses for the racetrack, and when I left school I helped him with them. We had six racehorses at that time, all of which were pretty successful, particularly Philco, who won a Group race. Alongside doing the racehorses, I was able to develop my competitive interests, which then were in showjumping. My first horse was an ex-racehorse called Barbarossa whom I took to Grade A.

I did do a bit of eventing through the Pony Club. The New Zealand Pony Club system is outstanding – everyone does a bit of everything and my parents got involved with helping, although they never pushed me. I was very keen, though, and lived and breathed riding, reading lots of books about it.

top *With Blodge, who I've momentarily managed to distract from mousing!*

above *Blodge has her eye on my ice-cream...*

'At the age of 21 I decided to see whether I could make it in the UK as a showjumper, and came over on a fact-finding mission ... but I didn't set the world on fire.'

Every night after school I would meet up with a group of kids and their ponies and we would hare about, galloping over fences on the neighbouring farms until well after dark.

My father was instrumental in getting good trainers into what was a pretty isolated area, one of whom at a later date was Lockie Richards, who was the first New Zealander to make an impact in eventing. Lockie was trainer to the squad for the Gawler World Championships in 1986 and he was particularly influential in my flatwork.

We also had a showjumping rider called David Murdoch, who helped me a lot and provided me with a horse called Speculate, already an established grand prix horse. David thought he would go well with a lighter rider and he gave me a great introduction to higher level.

I had lessons from the showjumper Kathy Kusner, and from the renowned American trainer George Morris, who both taught me to ride in a forward and rhythmic style, so that I learned a modern approach early on which stood me in good stead when I started eventing properly.

I was reasonably successful in showjumping, although very much in terms of the New Zealand circuit. I won two grands

'My first real foray into eventing came with an unlikely looking horse called Rata who was a chunky station-bred, but he was a good galloper and jumper.'

above More alternative transport – riding the mechanical rodeo bull at one of the Thirlestane's many great parties

left After the dressage at Burghley, 1992

opposite top With Rosemary Barlow, British fund-raiser extraordinaire and loyal New Zealand owner, at Stockholm in 1990

opposite bottom A 'chance ride' in the celebrity mounted games at Ston Easton in 1991

prix at Royal Shows, a puissance and a World Cup Pacific League qualifier. At the age of 21 I decided to see whether I could make it in the UK as a showjumper, and came over on a fact-finding mission with a horse called Mainspring – but I certainly didn't set the world on fire. I won a few competitions and had good placings at county shows and I had invaluable lessons from the late Caroline Bradley, but I didn't really know what I was doing and aimed far too big. However, my showjumping background has certainly played a large part in my eventing success.

My first real foray into eventing came with an unlikely looking horse called Rata who was

top *In front of the home crowd at Puhinui in 1994 where I clinched my second Land Rover World Rankings title*

above *Partying in Puhinui with (from left) Anna Hermann (now Hilton), Pippa Funnell, Carolyn Todd and Mary King*

a chunky station-bred, but he was a good galloper and jumper. My weakness was in dressage, which was an inevitable problem for me in the early days. If you're principally a showjumper, it is difficult to develop the right deep seat for dressage. Bill Noble, who has trained most of the leading New Zealand riders, taught me a lot at the higher levels, especially about having patience. This was particularly relevant with Messiah, who was a frustrating horse in the dressage phase.

Nowadays I still have help from Fiona Craig, a good dressage rider in her own right who is based in England. She is enormously supportive and she helped me through Atlanta and Rome. I have the odd showjumping lesson with Rodrigo Pessoa, the current World Champion, and Joe Fargis, but I also learn a lot both from my own experience and from watching my fellow competitors. I do quite a bit of teaching, time permitting, and it is something I might develop in future.

Teaching is an educational process for a rider, because you have to analyse and justify your reasoning and relate it to your own horses.

In those days New Zealand riders could go to championships with very little experience, and my placings with Rata in national competitions – we were always there or thereabouts, without doing anything fantastic – secured us a place on the squad for the 1986 World Championships in Gawler in Australia. Even that seemed a mammoth journey – although there is more opportunity for New Zealand riders to gain experience at the Australian events, people forget that flying in between these two countries is about the same as going from London to Moscow!

'Teaching is an educational process for a rider, because you have to analyse and justify your reasoning and relate it to your own horses.'

It was a terrible shock when Rata collapsed and died of cardiac arrest on the eve of the championships in Gawler. I was hacking him out with my team mate Andrew Scott and, while we were waiting for the British riders to finish their work, I cantered him slowly along a track.

below In Atlanta with France's Jean Teulere and Sally Clark

'Nowadays I still have help from Fiona Craig, a good dressage rider in her own right who is based in England. She is enormously supportive and she helped me through Atlanta and Rome.'

above Even Olympic champions have to clean their boots

right One of the most moving moments of my whole career – the walkabout at home after Atlanta

He suddenly veered off it, collapsed and seemed to lie there for ages, twitching. It was absolutely devastating and I felt that I'd never get over it, but the blunt truth is that if you're going to keep 'livestock', at some stage you're going to end up with 'deadstock' too. I can say this now, but at the time I'd never experienced anything like this before and it was terrible.

At that stage I didn't know anyone on the international eventing scene but the British team were fantastic. Clissy Strachan (now Bleekman) came straight over and hugged me and, in the midst of the tragedy, I did take on board that this sport really has a wonderful sense of camaraderie.

top Team bronze in Atlanta: another all-round New Zealand team effort

above With Sally Clark and Kerry Millikin after the individual competition in Atlanta

Some time later we were able to see the lighter side of things after Rata's poor owner, Louise McRae, who was only sixteen, was interviewed on TV. The first thing she said was that she 'loved her horse to death' and then, realising that didn't sound great, she said 'It was so unexpected – he's never done anything like this before!'

In fact, Gawler turned out to be absolutely disastrous for the New Zealand team. Mark Todd had a fall in the water with Charisma, but despite that we were still in the lead after cross-country with Tinks Pottinger in the individual gold position. But sadly her horse, Volunteer, failed the vets' inspection next morning due to a banged knee and that was the end of the team, although Trudy Boyce's unexpected great performance won the individual silver medal for us and showed that there might be more to come.

When I was growing up in New Zealand, eventing was a small sport. The three-day event was a rarity – certainly not something that happened every year – even now it is a relatively small circuit, with a spring and an autumn season and nothing in between. It was only when Mark Todd became so successful that it suddenly grew. His first Badminton win, in 1980 on Southern Comfort, was a great thrill, but it was his two successive Olympic gold medals on Charisma, in 1984 and 1988, which really gave the sport a kick at home.

above Paul O'Brien, with whom I share the yard, lungeing a new young horse, Dotcom

below The new generation: Haka, pictured as a four-year-old, of whom I have high hopes

Mark has always been very inspirational and helpful to my career, and when I first came to England both he and Andrew Nicholson gave me a lot of advice and were generous in their support. I'd like to think that I now help the younger riders coming to England.

Although we're very different types of people, we are all driven in the same way. The fact that the three of us – Mark, Andrew and I – have been the nucleus of the New Zealand team for so long is very special, and it is my greatest hope that we will all come together to be successful at the Sydney 2000 Olympics.

1 world champion MESSIAH

'Messiah was a precocious, confident character.'

Messiah was the horse who gave me the opportunity to make a career out of eventing and enabled me to prove that I was capable of performing at international level. Messiah was a 'professional': he thought of himself as an athlete, not a pet – and above all, he taught me that horses aren't machines. A horse's character can change during its career, and many become easier, but in Messiah's case, he became more difficult. His jumping and galloping were never in question, but he had a fragile temperament, and his performances in the dressage arena became more and more erratic.

'Messiah was a "professional": he thought of himself as an athlete, not a pet – and above all, he taught me that horses aren't machines.'

I was involved with Messiah right from the start because he was bred by a family friend, Carole Byles, who sent him to me as a three-year-old to back. Even then I thought he was a nice horse; he was very well balanced at an early stage, and could canter a 10m circle within the first few weeks. He was a precocious, confident character.

My relationship with him ended then because I was leaving New Zealand temporarily to showjump in Britain. Messiah was sent to Penny and Colin Macintosh to showjump and they produced him through to Grade B. But he was always a bit too forward-going to be a top showjumper, and tended to get into trouble in big combinations. At the same time, however, he wasn't suitable for speed competitions, as racing him against the clock would have blown his brains.

By 1986 I'd had my abortive trip to the World Three-day Event Championships in Gawler with Rata, and so it was suggested that I event Messiah. Carole had slight misgivings; Messiah was her baby and she adored him. She had hand-reared him – I always blamed her for his neuroses! – and she was worried that eventing was too gruelling a sport for him. But Messiah was

far left *A gold medal at Stockholm: the result that changed my life*

left *Our clear showjumping at Barcelona elevated us to individual bronze position*

below *Where it all started: Messiah at Taupo in 1988*

'Messiah was bred to gallop; he was an extravagant mover and an athletic jumper and very catlike on his feet – we never once fell.'

bred to gallop; he was an extravagant mover and an athletic jumper and very catlike on his feet – we never once fell.

We began our eventing career in 1987, our start having been delayed by my breaking a leg in a fall off a racehorse. He whipped up through the grades: in 1988 he finished 2nd in a bicentennial event in Sydney and first at Pukehohe three-day event. These results made me realise that to aim for the 1990 World Equestrian Games in Stockholm was not such a remote possibility.

It is a huge undertaking, both financially and emotionally, to cross the world with your horse. I felt there was no point getting to Stockholm just to have a look around; I wanted to be in with a chance. I had the support of the New Zealand selectors, I was 28 years old, and I felt that I was making a more mature decision than when I set sail at the age of 21 with the vague notion of becoming an international showjumper. I sold everything that wasn't nailed down, including my car and my guitar, and set off for Britain in May 1989, fully intending to return straight after the Games the following year.

I was based with the Monro family in Great Somerford, Wiltshire, and I will always be very grateful for the way they treated me as family. People were very friendly and welcoming to me when I arrived in England, and as it is part of the New Zealand culture to join in any party going, I found it easy to settle in. I never regretted my decision to come over, not even when things seemed desperately tough.

My first event in Britain was Longleat, where the top five placings in my class were taken by Kiwis: Mark Todd was 1st, Andrew Nicholson 2nd, myself 3rd, Bryce Newman 4th and Vaughn Jefferis 5th.

below *Messiah at Gatcombe in 1989, one of our very first competitions in England*

Our next outing was the CIC (international one-day event) at Chantilly in France, which was quite a culture shock. It seemed incredibly glamorous: there was a field of 70 and a huge arena in front of a beautiful chateau. Messiah coped easily and finished 2nd. I felt enormously relieved because this showed that he really was a good horse, and at least I felt my journey was completely justified. Burghley 1989 was out of the question, being a European Championship and closed to non-European riders – in hindsight this was probably a good thing for us – and so I ended up going to a three-day event at Achselschwang in Germany, where we finished 2nd, again, to Mark Todd on Bahlua.

Achselschwang was another education; it was the first time I'd seen such a naturally constructed course, using banks and other natural features. The steeplechase was very different from those in New Zealand, too, incorporating a hill and water. It was also the first time that I had travelled a horse a long distance overland to a competition, so that was another learning

above My first Badminton, in 1990: clearing the troubleome white rails into the Lake

curve. Messiah was still answering the questions as far as the jumping phases were concerned, but the dressage was definitely the weak link. This was partly my own problem too, due to my showjumping background, and I knew there was considerable room for improvement.

After spending the winter of 1989–90 back at home in New Zealand, I returned to Britain in the spring of 1990 to tackle my first Badminton. It was also my first four-star event and I hadn't even been to it as a spectator. However, Messiah won the advanced class at Brigstock that spring, which was a big, bold, pre-Badminton course and, with the blissful ignorance of the first-timer, I was full of confidence.

We were only about 23rd after dressage, but we had a great clear cross-country round, clocking up just 0.8 of a time penalty, over a shortened course which caused quite a bit of trouble that year, much of it to do with the very upright, bright white-painted rails into the Lake, which was sparkling in brilliant sunshine. We were 7th after cross-country, and thanks to a clear showjumping round, we not only finished on a score nearest to our dressage mark of anyone that year, but we were also 2nd – again! – this time to Nicky McIrvine (now Coe) on Middle Road.

Mark Phillips wrote in *Horse & Hound*: 'Blyth Tait and Messiah proved beyond all doubt what a class combination they are, even if they were a little lucky in the Lake. The New Zealand challenge in Stockholm continues to loom large.'

'I sold everything that wasn't nailed down, including my car and my guitar, and set off for Britain in May 1989 ...'

My father, who had never been to England before, came over to Badminton; it was in the days

when you could still bet on the bookies there, and he made quite a bit of money as I was priced at 33–1 each way! I was immediately made second favourite for Stockholm. Again, in my naïvety and incredible self-assuredness, this result only served to boost my confidence. Nicky McIrvine wasn't selected for the British team and, I reasoned, I had already beaten everyone else who was going! At that stage my whole life was consumed by thoughts of the World Championships. Ten years later, I can't believe that I was mad enough to be convinced that I would win. Now I am more likely to think it is 99–1 against!

'Nowadays I can't walk a major cross-country course without being stopped and asked what I think about a fence, or being filmed by a TV crew, or interviewed for radio.'

Looking back, I now realise that this was the last time I competed 'anonymously'. No one knew who I was, the press certainly weren't interested in my dressage test or what I thought of the course, and my name was constantly spelt and pronounced wrong, even in the programme!

Nowadays I can't walk a major cross-country course without being stopped and asked what I think about a fence, or filmed by a TV crew, or interviewed for radio. Finding the actual time for this sort of thing is a greater problem than the pressure of the attention. Any rider who can't cope with this attention is going to have a problem, because if you want to get to the top you have to realise that giving interviews and press conferences is part and parcel of it – it helps develop and maintain the profile of the sport, which is needed to get sponsorship and recognition.

opposite *Messiah showjumps clear en route to finishing 2nd at his Badminton debut*

The worst thing about being interviewed regularly is that sometimes you're going to get it wrong, and I have certainly said many things I regret. I've been misquoted and taken out of context, which I used to find upsetting, but I've got used to it because it soon gets forgotten. My worst quotes have usually been taken from something I have said in the heat of the moment, probably because I'm extremely disappointed and haven't stopped to think what it will sound like on paper.

New Zealand had its first really strong squad to choose from for Stockholm, with Mark Todd, Andrew Nicholson, Tinks Pottinger, Vicky Latta, Vaughn Jefferis and Andrew Scott, all of whom had competed in Europe with distinction. However, I was confident of being chosen for the team.

Financial support for the team has increased in ratio to our results over the years, but even then masses of enthusiastic supporters came and helped, considering that the competition was so far from home. We had our own supporters' tent and it was great fun. I couldn't have wished to have been part of a better team in Stockholm. We are all very different people, but we do come together well as a team – there are no internal politics and it's always a great atmosphere. Mark is largely responsible for this and he and Andrew Nicholson led the way on this occasion.

Once we'd walked the course, I thought 'great', because it was long – the optimum time was over 13 minutes – twisty and turning. I knew it would suit Messiah as he was the sort of horse who could probably have won a

MESSIAH

BORN	1979
OWNER/ BREEDER	Carole Byles
BREEDING	NZ Thoroughbred by Abalou out of Portia
COLOUR	Brown
HEIGHT	16hh

Career highlights

1989	2nd Achselschwang, 2nd Chantilly
1990	2nd Badminton, 1st individual and team gold Stockholm World Championships
1992	11th Saumur, 3rd final team trial, 3rd and team silver Barcelona Olympics

'It was hot and humid, but New Zealand horses generally thrive in the heat – they don't like the wet and cold, and don't go well in it – and neither do I!'

right Messiah passed the trot-up at Stockholm with no trouble at all

below Dressage at Stockholm: Mark Phillips wrote in Horse & Hound 'Blyth Tait and Messiah finally produced the test they had been threatening all summer'

steeplechase. He did have a tendency to chuck his head about, but he could be turned easily and he was an effortless galloper.

I was given the third spot in the team, which meant that I had a day's grace in the dressage to settle him, in which I grazed him by the arena and lunged him. It also meant that our test took place in the relative quiet of the morning. Afterwards we were lying 6th; Messiah had excelled himself and I felt a different person afterwards because I knew that we were well on our way from there. This time Mark Phillips wrote: 'Blyth Tait and Messiah finally produced the test they had been threatening all summer'!

If I am to get nervous at an event, it will be before the dressage. Even though this phase has become so crucial nowadays, I will still choose a horse that is first and foremost a good jumping Thoroughbred, and this does sometimes leave me open to problems with the dressage.

Andrew Nicholson went first across country, and completed clear and inside the time on Spinning Rhombus. Andrew is a true professional; he is well known for his ability as a trailblazer, and this is where he has made such a significant contribution to New Zealand's team success. His information is always useful. At Stockholm he told me not to panic if I was down on time early on the course, as I'd be able to make it up further on, which was something I was worried about. In fact, Messiah came thundering home as if he'd just started out. It was hot and humid, but New Zealand horses generally thrive in the heat – they don't like the wet and cold, and don't go well in it – and neither do I!

I remember the Stockholm course as being hard work, as it was long, and I'm sure our round wasn't copybook, but it really was one of those great cross-country rides. I finished in the lead with Didier Seguret of France lying 2nd, and Andrew 3rd – the three of us were the only ones to complete within the time. Messiah was quite sound next day – he had legs of steel – and such was my naïvety that it never occurred to me then that my horse wouldn't be sound enough to showjump!

'Messiah was quite sound next day – he had legs of steel – and such was my naïvety that it never occurred to me then that my horse wouldn't be sound enough to showjump!'

This phase was never going to be a problem because Messiah was virtually a Grade A showjumper and he hadn't knocked a fence down all season in England. Poor Didier had a

below I knew the course at Stockholm would suit Messiah

above A fantastic day for New Zealand: team gold in Stockholm. (from left) Andrew Scott on Umptee; myself; Andrew Nicholson on Spinning Rhombus; and Mark Todd on Bahlua; with our chef d'équipe, Denis Pain

nightmare round with six fences down, and Andrew had three down, which dropped him to 4th behind Ian Stark on Murphy Himself and Bruce Davidson on Pirate Lion.

I went into the arena knowing that I had at least a rail in hand. We did in fact have the last fence down, because as he came to jump it, the crowd erupted and this startled Messiah so that he shot forwards, catching it with his hindlegs. Mark Todd finished 5th and Andrew Scott 14th on Umptee and we beat Britain to team gold by over 40 penalties! Our individuals, Vicky Latta with Chief and Vaughn Jefferis with Enterprise, finished 11th and 22nd as well, so there were huge celebrations in Stockholm and the party lasted for quite a while!

I have since been lucky enough to find out that the significance of winning a major title doesn't hit you at once. Of course you're ecstatic at the time, but the real meaning doesn't sink in for a while. In my naïvety then, this title didn't really change my way of thinking. I suppose that if I'd fallen off in Stockholm I would have gone straight home; instead it proved the catalyst for changing my life. The 1992 Barcelona Olympics were looming, I had brought Ricochet over to England as my second string, and I was enjoying myself immensely, so decided to stay on.

'This phase was never going to be a problem because Messiah was virtually a Grade A showjumper and he hadn't knocked a fence down all season in England.'

However, the next year – 1991 – was a different story, which is so typical of this sport. It was my first taste of how things can go badly wrong in eventing. Messiah and I won a few one-day events in the spring, and we arrived at Badminton expecting to win that too. We were greeted with a new-found interest, due to being world champions, and all the journalists previewed the competition as a clear-cut battle between Ginny Elliot and myself. How wrong they were!

When I went out to warm up for dressage I was greeted by a startling barrage of photographers. This, combined with the whole Badminton atmosphere, soon made Messiah completely

below left *Messiah about to blow up in the dressage at Badminton in 1991*

below *At the South of England horse trials in 1991*

bottom *Messiah on his way to victory in an advanced class at Belton in 1991*

'I was starting to have problems with Messiah's temperament ... he seemed to be constantly looking for an opportunity to be awkward ...'

over-excited, and when we finally went into the arena for our test he started leaping sideways up the centre line. He messed around so much during his test that he struck into himself at the back of the tendon sheath and had to be withdrawn. End of story. We didn't even do another three-day event that year.

The following spring, 1992, for our Olympic preparation we decided against Badminton, which proved a blessing because it was so wet, and went instead to the three-star event at Saumur in France. I was number one to go, and although I was happy about this, the better dressage marks obviously came later. The course wasn't overly stiff, but Messiah went well and I was pleased. We were 11th and qualified for Barcelona.

By this stage I was starting to have problems with Messiah's temperament. He'd had 1991 off, but the excitement of Stockholm had had an effect. He was always fine at home, but he seemed to be constantly looking for an opportunity to be awkward at events and he was starting to get the better of me in the dressage. He was still going well across country, but he would blow up in the arena. However, we were 3rd in the final trial at Savernake – I also won on Delta and Richochet – and were thus selected for the New Zealand team for Barcelona.

below *Messiah was the ultimate athlete*

I was torn between riding Messiah and Ricochet, who had won Punchestown and who was going at his very best, so I took them both to Barcelona. But as I walked the course, I knew that it was a track for Messiah. The distances were on long strides, it was a course for a bold, galloping horse, and it had his name written all over it.

However, it wasn't long before we were caught up in another major drama. I was riding along the track between the training area and stables when an earth-moving machine came towards us. Messiah started jumping about, and managed to tread on a sharp stone. He limped a bit, but then appeared to get over it; however, I warned our team vet Wally Neiderer about it. We kept an eye out for bruising, and on the day of the first trot-up we took precautions, tubbing Messiah's foot and taking the shoe off. He passed and all seemed well ... until an hour before our dressage test! As we trotted up towards the arena he was definitely lame. All hell broke loose: we took the shoe off, then the pad off – and he was still lame. We tweaked the pad, and he was no better.

I was getting peculiar looks from everyone around because I was due into the dressage arena and wasn't on the horse yet. I was getting into a real state – but, as usual, the New Zealand team rallied around, and Andrew Nicholson was at his best. He said: 'Look, this is the point of no return.

'I went straight into the arena and suddenly Messiah seemed to realise that he was the centre of the drama. He felt immediately very alive. As we cantered down the centre line in the arena it dawned on him that he was there solely to show off.'

left Messiah showing off in the dressage at Barcelona

No one expects you to do more than you can.'

So there was nothing for it but to get on with it. I went straight into the arena and suddenly Messiah seemed to realise that he was the centre of the drama. He felt immediately very alive. As we cantered down the centre line in the arena it dawned on him that he was there solely to show off. From that moment on he certainly didn't look lame, mainly because he refused to take a single step of trot! His behaviour was appalling and we finished nearly bottom on a mark of 78.8, over 30 marks behind the leader, Germany's Matthias Baumann.

I was absolutely devastated and felt that the whole thing just wasn't worth it; but again, the

'Messiah jumped and galloped with ease; at the 11-minute marker he was up on time and I was starting to feel really excited. However, nothing is that simple ...'

Kiwi team sprang into action. They all said: 'Look, there's a day and a half to go before cross-country and we'll sort it out. Just have a go.'

So we tubbed and relieved Messiah's foot again, knowing that it really was only a stone bruise, and by the time we had to trot in front of a veterinary panel on cross-country morning he was fine. The ground jury said: 'It's your decision, but we'll be keeping a close eye!' but as I was in the team I felt I had to try to start. Amazingly, Messiah didn't take one single lame step from the start of Phase A; I suppose the galloping brought fresh blood to the area.

As the cross-country phase progressed I became aware of the toll it was taking. Andrew was first to go for our team, and by the time I set out he was still in the lead – and *his* dressage mark hadn't been brilliant! In fact, my seemingly hopeless dressage score turned out to be better than most of the finishers! It was clear that I would have to have a go.

Messiah jumped and galloped with ease; at the 11-minute marker he was up on time and I was starting to feel really excited. However, nothing is that simple and, sure enough, we had another almost farcical drama: there was a combination near the end of the course with a waggon to an oxer on a related distance followed by a tight turn. We were going too fast and came in too close to the second element; Messiah was starting to slip on the turn and I was trying to steady him – but he thought I was trying to set him up for the barrier which was deemed unjumpable and was there to stop people taking it on – so he took off

below *After our disastrous dressage we just had to go for it*

left *Messiah just before we dramatically left the course*

below *Barcelona was a course for a bold galloping horse, and had Messiah's name written all over it*

'Next day Messiah jumped his usual clear showjumping round – and suddenly we had won an individual bronze medal!'

over it. Suddenly I found myself in the ridiculous situation of being off the course and in the middle of some trees! We ended up having to gallop down a track to get back on the course, and this cost us about seven time penalties.

It was very frustrating but we still went into 8th place with the second fastest time. Matt Ryan was fastest on Kibah Tic Toc and went into the lead, and Andrew, who had the third fastest time, was in silver medal position. The New Zealand team was easily in the lead, despite Mark having pulled up lame on Welton Greylag, and Vicky Latta having had a misfortune with a badly marked penalty zone – this was ultimately to cost her a medal. Next day Messiah jumped his usual clear showjumping round – and suddenly we had won an individual bronze medal! In view of how the event had started for us, it was a good lesson in thinking before throwing the toys out of the pram.

It was amazing, really, that we took home team silver. All four of us had had a disaster: Andrew had a demoralising showjumping round with nine fences down which cost him an individual medal and us team gold, but he had been the team trailblazer who had boosted everyone's confidence. If Vicky hadn't missed the penalty zone, we'd have won; if Mark's horse hadn't gone lame we'd have won, and he might have won his third successive individual gold medal; and if I'd have done just a *normal*, never mind good, dressage test we'd have won – so it was very much an all-round team performance.

In hindsight, that was the moment at which I should have retired Messiah. He nearly blew his brains out in the medal ceremony, and his girl groom Delayne Cooke and Mike Tucker between them really had their hands full just trying to hold him.

below *Who'd have believed it? Receiving my medal from the Princess Royal*

By the spring of 1993 he was very awkward in his lack of submission and unwillingness to listen and work on the flat. When I first rode him he was good at dressage, but the combination of the spectators and the general palaver of big events gave him the excuse to show that he wasn't normal. By this stage he was 14, and we didn't do another three-day event – I felt that he'd done enough great things, and he'd always given of his best. He went home to Carole, who hunted him, and he gave her a comfortable ride because he was enjoying himself doing his own thing and not being disciplined. He is still happy and well, and still being hacked about by Carole.

Messiah was certainly the horse who at the time gave me the greatest opportunity. But he needed individual attention – he wasn't a team player – and if I was offered him now, I probably wouldn't accept him because he would need too much work. It was right that he was my only horse in those days, and we had very much a one-to-one relationship, which worked.

He certainly influenced my riding style and technique, especially because he was always very nervous of water – he would leap into it like

'In hindsight, that was the moment at which I should have retired Messiah. He nearly blew his brains out in the medal ceremony, and his girl groom Delayne Cooke and Mike Tucker between them really had their hands full just trying to hold him.'

left *Delayne Cooke hangs onto Messiah for grim death at the medal ceremony in Barcelona*

the launch of the *Titanic*, and would bolt through. He was really quite wild! All I could do was stick at it and persevere, and eventually my faith was justified because he took both the direct routes at water at the Barcelona Olympics, and was one of few horses to do so. But at Stockholm he was too bold and forward, and nearly got too close to the bank in the water complex there, and it was only because he was such an exceptional cross-country horse that he got himself out of trouble.

I spent many hours trying to get him accustomed to water, and I just hoped he would improve with experience, but he was always pretty hairy at water fences, right up to the end of his eventing career. He was very difficult to sit on into water, and, as a result, he is entirely responsible for my now well-known exaggerated backward position when jumping into water on any horse. If I was to try anything else I think I'd fall off, so I'm stuck with it now!

above *Messiah with Stockholm groom Fiona McMeeken*

2 big bold galloping RICOCHET

'Ricochet was one of the loveliest horses to train and he deserves his own chapter just for his consistency ...'

above *Ricochet with his previous rider, Mary Darby, at Mata Awa one-day event in 1989*

Ricochet was one of the loveliest horses to train and he deserves his own chapter just for his consistency, but because he perhaps lacked that edge of brilliance he tended to live slightly in Messiah's shadow; as a result, he was never given a championship opportunity. He travelled all the way to the Barcelona Olympics only to end up having a Spanish holiday instead because I decided to ride Messiah, despite the fact that he had shown the better pre-Olympic form of the two.

Ric was the first 'made'' horse I had ever ridden, and also, at an upstanding 16.2hh, one of the biggest. I got him when I had returned from my first eventing season in England to ride some novice horses I had at home in New Zealand; I was planning to take them back to the UK with me because I felt that, in having only Messiah in Europe, all my eggs were in one basket – but I ended up selling them all to buy Ricochet. He was then 11, and was owned by Mayling Dillon and Mary Darby, who is now our chairman of selectors. Mary had won both the novice and intermediate championships at home, but was finding him quite strong. She suggested I ride him at the Pukehohe three-day event at the end of 1989 and we finished an encouraging

'Ric was the first "made" horse I had ever ridden, and also, at an upstanding 16.2hh, one of the biggest.'

'I was particularly pleased about these results because I felt it proved to me that I wasn't just a one-horse rider.'

RICOCHET

BORN	1977
BREEDING	NZ TB by Take A Risk
COLOUR	Bay
HEIGHT	16.2hh

Career highlights

1989	3rd Pukehohe
1990	4th Chantilly, 5th British Open at Gatcombe, 1st Scottish Open Championships, 5th Burghley
1992	1st Punchestown, 1st final Olympic trial at Savernake, reserve horse for NZ Olympic team, 1st Scottish Open Championships, 6th Blenheim
1993	3rd Al Poplar Park, 1st advanced Ston Easton, 2nd Badminton

above *Ricochet at Gatcombe in 1990*

3rd, which earned Ric a longlisting for the Stockholm World Games as my second string.

It wasn't until I got back from all the razzmattazz of Stockholm in the summer of 1990 that Ric got his first chance to star. Thirlestane Castle in Scotland was just his sort of track – big, bold and galloping and on great going – and we won the Scottish Championships there before going on to finish 5th at Burghley. I was particularly pleased about these results because I felt it proved to me that I wasn't just a one-horse rider. Ric was only the second horse I had ridden at four-star level and a good placing at Burghley made me more confident that I really was competitive at that level.

Ricochet's results that summer were also helpful in my search for sponsorship. My first real supporters then were Peter and Ginny Vaughan: I met them through Ian Mackenzie, a long-time owner and friend, and they sponsored me in a small and friendly way through their company Countrywide Surveyors; they had three pony-mad daughters and were excited to be involved in the sport of eventing. The Vaughans became very much my 'family' in England, and they provided fantastic support.

'Few people probably have any idea of the problems that we foreign riders encounter when we first come over to England ...'

Few people probably have any idea of the problems that we foreign riders encounter when we first come over to England: for instance, how do you travel your horse to an event, and where do you find, say, some showjumps to school over? And if you already have a house at home in New Zealand it's unlikely that you will be able to afford, for example, a second washing machines, so how do you get your clothes washed? How do you run two cars on either side of the world? At that stage I was sharing a tiny cottage with Jo Shepherd and Paul O'Brien and we had only one car between us, which Paul later crashed! On this occasion Peter (Vaughan) lent me the lorry he used in the hunting season so I could travel the horses to events. All in all it was the Vaughan family's kindness and involvement that helped solve all these small but important practical problems, and made life a lot easier for me.

Due to a minor injury, Ricochet missed 1991 – as I mentioned in Messiah's chapter, 1991

below Ricochet gets his chance to shine in 1990 and finishes 5th at Burghley

above *A good day's work at Badminton: Delta and Ricochet*

was altogether rather a non-event for me. But in the spring of that year I learnt a big lesson with Ricochet. I thought I had it all sussed as far as preparing a horse was concerned, but on this occasion I was guilty of trying to be too regimented. I had worked out a canter programme for Ric and was determined to stick to it, but I didn't take into account the fact that the ground was very deep that spring – it was my first real experience of bottomless going. Basically I worked him too hard in the mud, and as a result he incurred a slight strain to a front tendon. I gave him the rest of the year off and he came back for 1992 after a slow build-up through the winter, for which the credit must go to Hamish, Muffet and Alexander Monro, who worked him while I was in New Zealand. It was my first real experience of a soundness problem, but I learned a lot as a result and I now know that nine out of ten problems with legs can be prevented.

'It was my first real experience of a soundness problem, but I learned a lot as a result and I now know that nine out of ten problems with legs can be prevented.'

Ricochet was always rather an 'old' horse. He could be crotchety and stiff, and he never trotted up well after the cross-country phase of an event. He never exploded when you turned him out, but would just amble off and graze. Even so, he was quite a character, and could be quite smart – and he would try things on, too. At Punchestown he suddenly decided, to my horror, that he would hang his tongue out of the side of his mouth. I rushed off to find a Fulmer bit to correct him – but then he stopped doing it as suddenly as he had started it, and never did it again!

'... he never worked against you and always tried to please, so he was usually up among the leaders after dressage.'

Ric was not particularly athletic or scopey, nor was he the most talented horse, and his way of going across country certainly wasn't copybook – he reminded me of Andrew Nicholson's horse Spinning Rhombus in the way he would just get on with it without doing anything spectacular. However, he was actually very capable in all three phases, and in particular would always do a good showjumping round – there was no weak link. Also he never worked against you and always tried to please, so he was usually up among the leaders after dressage.

His first career was as a somewhat unsuccessful racehorse – his track name was Risk It – but I was surprised to read that his trainer had found him difficult to deal with. He was similar to Chesterfield, in that he was very sweet-natured and never dreamed of kicking or biting. But he wasn't up to a heavy workload and, because of Messiah, he was never really number one; also,

below *Ricochet at full stretch over the footbridge at Thirlestane on his way to winning in 1992*

> **'I was in a quandary about Barcelona, because Ric had the better current form of the two, but he was strong and tended to hang rather on corners, and although he was a good galloper, he didn't have the scope of Messiah.'**

by the time he did qualify as my lead horse, he was too old.

In 1992 Ric gave me my first win in Ireland, at Punchestown. I always get vibes when I arrive at a three-day event as to whether it's going to be a good one or whether it will be unremarkable, and as soon as I saw Punchestown I knew I was going to love it. It is surrounded by lovely green hills which always remind me of New Zealand, and in those days the cross-country course was a big, imposing galloping track which suited Ricochet down to the ground; now it has become more technical. Needless to say, there is always a great Irish welcome at Punchestown: it is everything a three-day event should be. And of course the Irish claimed our win as an Irish victory – 'Rick O'Shea'!

Ric went on to win a competitive advanced section at Savernake, where several nations were having their final Olympic trial, and I took him out to Barcelona with Messiah. I was in a quandary,

above left & above *Ricochet finished 2nd at Badminton in 1993, but it was one of the hairiest rounds of my life*

left *A clear round at Blenheim pulls us back up to 6th place in 1992 after one of his rare cross-country mistakes*

above Another rather hairy moment at Badminton

because Ric had the better current form of the two, but he was strong and tended to hang rather on corners, and although he was a good galloper, he didn't have the scope of Messiah.

As it had been a big year, when we got home I opted for Blenheim instead of Burghley that autumn. At this event we were lying in 2nd place after the dressage, but he put in an uncharacteristic sharp run-out at the complex in the main arena, which was three progressively narrowing arrowheads; in fact this is the only penalty of any significance that I can remember him incurring. But with a clear showjumping round we pulled up four places to 6th, which was an amazing result considering we had had a stop – another case of 'if only'.

I ran Ric only once at Badminton, in 1993 when he was 15, and he finished 2nd, but it was one of the hairiest rounds of my life. Earlier in the day Delta had given me a fabulous, foot-perfect round, so perhaps I was lulled into a false sense of security. In short, Ric gave me one of the most chaotic cross-country rides I've ever had. He was very strong and didn't like having to be set up for fences, so he just took strides out where he felt like it and put them in where he shouldn't have. Coming back through Huntsman's Close

'He was very strong and didn't like having to be set up for fences, so he just took strides out where he felt like it and put them in where he shouldn't have.'

where there was an angled log, bank combination, he somehow bounced the stride prior to the bank and squeezed in a stride on top of the bank, where he shouldn't have taken a stride! I was struggling to keep up to the optimum time because I was wasting valuable seconds having to manoeuvre him and set him up for fences, and by the time we approached the finish I was kicking and flapping and shoving to get him home – but somehow we finished bang on the optimum time. We won the Omega watch for doing so, and Mike Tucker, who was commentating, raved about my 'great judgement'; but in fact it had been a real struggle, and had a lot more to do with good luck! This was the second of my three runner-up placings at Badminton. Ginny Elliot won it on Welton Houdini, having done an infinitely better cross-country than me, but we finished only 1.8 dressage marks behind her.

above *Another 2nd place at Badminton, in 1993 – Princess Michael of Kent presents me with the Omega watch*

After that Ric was retired and I gave him to Candy Sellick, an expatriate New Zealander who lives in Hampshire; Ric must think he has died and gone to heaven, she looks after him so well. He is a horse who needs a lot of loving, and I tease Candy about the bald patch on his neck where she has patted him so much! He celebrated his 21st birthday last year, and looks fantastic; he still enjoys competing in riding club competitions with Candy.

below *Ric looks the picture of health on his 21st birthday*

3 flying fences on DELTA

Delta was a fantastic mare, and she gave me the best cross-country ride I have ever had in my life to date; but at home she was a complete nuisance. I particularly remember one day when I was based at Soley Farm near Hungerford and my groom Delayne Cooke and I were both under pressure in pouring rain to get ten horses done for the night on our own before darkness fell. But as was her wont, Delta chose to pull back sharply and escape. She

made purposefully for the narrow exit out of the barn, and trotted down the road towards Chilton Foliat village and the main A4 road with us in hot pursuit, merrily jumping in and out of people's fields and gardens. She wasn't galloping, she was mischievously, and frustratingly, keeping just out of reach – it was two hours before we could catch her.

My friend Jo Shepherd produced Delta, and first brought the mare over to England when she came to join Paul and me. Right from the start Delta was always pulling back, breaking ropes, pulling hooks out of walls and careering around the garden. I used to pull my hair out in exasperation and would harangue Jo: 'For God's sake get your horse under control!' – but I have to admit that when I had Delta myself later on she was just as bad! Even now she still hasn't lost her 'bush pony' attitutude: often when I ask Jo how she is, she says: 'I don't know, I haven't laid a hand on her for four months!'

'... she gave me the best cross-country ride I have ever had in my life to date; but at home she was a complete nuisance.'

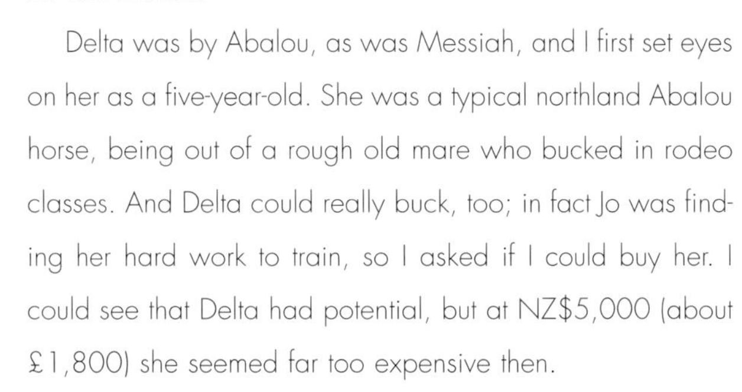

Delta was by Abalou, as was Messiah, and I first set eyes on her as a five-year-old. She was a typical northland Abalou horse, being out of a rough old mare who bucked in rodeo classes. And Delta could really buck, too; in fact Jo was finding her hard work to train, so I asked if I could buy her. I could see that Delta had potential, but at NZ$5,000 (about £1,800) she seemed far too expensive then.

Jo is an independent, hard-working person and she decided it was worth bringing Delta to England to compete, so she came and based herself with me and worked in English pubs to finance the trip. They did fairly well to start with and were placed in quite a few advanced classes; but they then went to Bramham in a year when it was pouring with rain and had a fall jumping up out of a sunken road complex. Delta struck into the back of her leg and damaged a tendon, so Jo went home and left Delta with me. She came back the following year but Delta's leg was still throwing out warning signs and, as Jo couldn't afford to stay in England if she wasn't competing properly, she decided to go home. She had put everything into coming to England with Delta, but it seemed that it just wasn't meant to be – and Jo's case is a classic example of the risk that foreigners face when they decide to make the break.

As soon as I started riding Delta I knew she was talented. Jo wanted to sell her but I couldn't afford to buy her on the open market, so I suggested we organise a syndicate in which Jo had one share, with the proviso that she had the

DELTA

BORN	1980
BREEDING	By Abalou (NZ TB) out of a rodeo mare
BREEDER	Joanna Shepherd
OWNERS	A syndicate – Jo Shepherd, Ian Mackenzie, Barbara Thomson, Noelle McNaught and myself
COLOUR	Bay
HEIGHT	16hh

Career highlights

1992	1st final Olympic trial, 2nd Burghley
1993	15th Badminton
1994	2nd Badminton, 1st WEG final trials at Althorp, 1st Scottish Open Championship

left Delta with Jo Shepherd, who produced her, at Pukehohe in 1986

mare back to breed from. Jo has always been a fantastic friend to me as she could have got far more for Delta on the open market but she wanted me to have the opportunity, so she agreed, and I arranged a syndicate between Noelle McNaught, a wonderful horse-loving lady from Wanganui, Ian Mackenzie and Barbara Thomson, New Zealand's leading equestrian photographer.

Our first three-day event was in the spring of 1992 at Saumur, where we finished 13th on

our dressage score. Then at the final trial for the World Championships at Savernake, Delta convincingly won an advanced section – as did Ricochet – and in the autumn we were 2nd at Burghley. At first Delta and I were at loggerheads in the dressage and it took me some time to achieve the same partnership Jo had had with her in this phase. At Burghley we were way down the order after the dressage, in 45th place in fact, which seemed hopeless, but it was a year in which the cross-country time was very difficult to attain – the only partnership to do

'As soon as I started riding Delta I knew she was talented. Jo wanted to sell her but I couldn't afford to buy her on the open market, so I suggested we organise a syndicate in which Jo had one share, with the proviso that she had the mare back to breed from.'

left *Delta shows her scope at our first three-day event, Saumur, in 1992*

'... Delta hardly ever touched a showjump – but on this occasion of course we had our first one down, a triple bar would you believe ...'

so was Brynley Powell with Spiderman. Delta and I were only four seconds over the time, so we moved up to third place behind him and Charlotte Bathe with The Cool Customer. Bryn had two showjumps down and dropped to 5th, and Charlotte didn't have a fence in hand over us: victory was therefore within reach, as Delta hardly ever touched a showjump – but on this occasion of course we had our first one down, a triple bar would you believe, which gave Charlotte the leeway to have one down too. This win was a tremendous result for Charlotte – she is a good friend, and it

__below__ Delta's fantastic cross-country round at Burghley in 1992 elevated us from 45th place after the dressage to 2nd

above *Burghley 1992, where unusually Delta had a showjump down which kept us in 2nd*

far left *The expression says it all: dressage was always Delta's Achilles' heel*

left *With Burghley winner Charlotte Hollingsworth (now Bathe) and 3rd-placed Tina Gifford (left)*

'I had the most fantastic cross-country round on Delta that year; indeed seven years later it still rates as my ultimate ride.'

was the breakthrough she needed for her career, so I was really pleased for her.

Dressage continued to be our Achilles' heel. At Badminton in 1993 we were way down the scoreboard after the dressage, in the bottom twenty of the field. I was drawn first to go, something which was definitely not helpful. In fact I don't mind at all being first to go across country, and if you ride two horses at a three-day event it is something you have to be prepared for.

I had the most fantastic cross-country round on Delta that year; indeed seven years later it still rates as my ultimate ride. My round on Ready Teddy at Atlanta was probably the next most memorable, but it wasn't copybook, whereas Delta was absolutely perfect throughout. We pulled up to 15th eventually.

If you lined up all my six best horses on the flat for a straight galloping race Delta would come last, but she was the fastest of all over fences because she was so easy to ride. I rode her in a snaffle, and never had to take a pull before a fence because she was so clever and could just jump straight

right Delta gives me the best ride of my life at Badminton in 1993

below Delta at the start of the Badminton steeplechase

out of her stride, no matter what the question. I would take risks on her and fly into fences that I would never tackle in the same way on any other horse.

The next year, 1994, we finished 2nd at Badminton and were part of a New Zealand one-two-three with Mark Todd on Horton Point and Vaughn Jefferis on Bounce. It was hard to come so close again at Badminton, and as Mark had only taken the ride on Horton Point the day before the competition started, I couldn't help wishing he'd stayed home on this occasion! But you couldn't take any of the credit away from Mark – Horton Point was a totally strange horse to him and he was drawn first to go, so it was just an incredible piece of horsemanship; and the whole New Zealand sweep was wonderful for our supporters.

It is still a regret that Delta never actually won a major competition – she came so close at both Badminton and Burghley – because she was such a superb cross-country horse. If I had understood her dressage deficiencies sooner, it might have been a different story, but she had too much of her mother, the rodeo mare, in her. I did eventually persuade her to become more rounded in shape and more forward going, but when I tried to get her to give more, she couldn't, and all I would get was crookedness and resistance.

above *I still regret that Delta never won a major competition – on our way to another near miss, at Badminton in 1994*

right *I felt so confident after our test in The Hague ...*

I had to learn to accentuate her strong points and not try to make her do what she simply couldn't do. Before The Hague, Fiona Craig, who has helped me a great deal over the last six years, made me go right back to basics and helped me to get her more supple and fluent. This made a huge difference to our dressage results in our last year together.

Another problem with Delta was that she was very cold-backed, and she would try to buck you off if she hadn't been ridden for a while. You could never just get straight on her, especially after a break in work. We would have to lead her around first with the saddle on and even then she would plant her feet and threaten to buck. She was a great character with a real mind of her own.

In 1994 the final team trial for the World Championships was held at a smart new event at Althorp, and Delta won here, too; it was therefore no surprise that New Zealand went to the championships in The Hague in Holland as favourites, with Delta and me joint favourites with Mark Todd on Just An Ace to win the individual title. By this stage I had a full sponsorship from the clothing company Toggi, and was in constant demand for magazine interviews. Toggi was also very generously sponsoring the whole New Zealand team that year, so expectations were justifiably very high.

'If you lined up all my six best horses on the flat for a straight galloping race Delta would come last, but she was the fastest of all over fences because she was so easy to ride.'

In .the team were the three of us from the Badminton

225
N.Z.

'... and when Delta and I were lying 6th after dressage, I was convinced that we'd win – by a weird coincidence I've been 6th after dressage at all three world championships.'

one-two-three, with the addition of Andrew Nicholson on the bold jumper Jagermeister, the reigning British intermediate champions; this meant there was no place on the team for Vicky Latta, who was very disappointed to have to run as an individual. However, against all predictions and not inconsiderable hype, The Hague turned out to be a disaster for New Zealand, with three out of the team ending up on the floor.

I was third to go for the team, and when Delta and I were lying 6th after dressage, I was convinced that we'd win – by a weird coincidence I've been 6th after dressage at all three world championships. But it was not to be, for several reasons. Delta, despite all her other quirks, has never suffered from 'mareish' problems – except in The Hague, and what a time to pick! Also, the weather was very hot and humid, and this took the Dutch organising team, as well as everyone else, very much by surprise. Cross-country day was already a logistical nightmare, and involved taking a day off after dressage to transfer to the course, which was a couple of hours away in dense scrub forest. Only extremely rudimentary facilities were provided, which was especially hard on the poor grooms – for instance there was just one loo for everyone, and bottled water cost £6.50 a litre; really the organisation which prevailed at these championships was fairly chaotic.

Delta was usually so bright, and she had a terrific engine, but on Phase C she got muscle cramp and got slower and slower, possibly related to her being in season. It was very hot and the track was through deep sand; it looped away from the stables for the last bit and I actually had to whack Delta to keep her going. When we arrived in the ten-minute box I obviously told Wally Neiderer, our team vet, what had happened; yet when he took her temperature and heart rate he found both were perfectly all right.

By this stage in the competition Vaughn had had a fantastic round on Bounce and was in the lead, but Andrew had had an unexpected fall on Jagermeister, who had tripped coming out of a water complex. I felt I had to have a go, both for the sake of the team and for the defence of my title. But Delta literally stumbled out of the start box. She did then pick herself up and jump the first few fences really quite cleanly; but at fence six you had to jump over a ditch and push up on to a bank, and here she just couldn't cope. She got stuck, and

right Delta leaves England on a winning note: jumping the massive footbridge in cold blood at Thirlestane in 1994

lay on the bank without the strength to haul herself up, and unable to touch the ground with her hindlegs either. It was an awful, distressing moment and obviously I called it a day and retired. As usual the team was very understanding, but the New Zealand press was fairly unhelpful and wanted to know why on earth I hadn't carried on.

'It was very hot and the track was through deep sand; it looped away from the stables for the last bit and I actually had to whack Delta to keep her going.'

Things went from bad to worse: Mark Todd, who by this stage was in with a chance of at least an individual medal, if not the title, had a fall at the same fence as Andrew, and Vicky Latta had a run-out with Chief. Thankfully, Vaughn saved face for New Zealand and rescued the individual title, which at least gave our support group, who had travelled a long way, something to cheer about. Needless to say, I was extremely disappointed: it was one of the

'... I was in a position to win, so I thought "What the hell!" and picked Delta up – and she just flew it as if it was a Pony Club fence!'

biggest blows I have had to absorb, and the fact that we'd gone out as favourites and ended up on the floor so early on made it even worse.

However, you are only as good as your last result, so when something like this happens all you can do is pick yourself up and carry on. It was still a good year: I won the 1994 Land Rover World Rankings, having won it in 1992, and I won Bramham and Boekelo with Aspyring. Andrew also picked himself up and won Achselschwang, and he was the national points champion again. We were perhaps lucky as a nation that there was no accusatory post mortem in the national press at home, and no suggestion that New Zealanders were finished as an eventing nation, or that we should drastically change officials or training, as happens in some other countries in the wake of disaster. It was just considered a major disappointment.

The plan was to retire Delta at this point. She was only 13, but she had a mildly degenerative joint disease in a front fetlock, and the plan was to send her home to breed from. However, when we got back from The Hague, entries were still open for Thirlestane, which had been a successful and happy event for me, and so I decided to give her one last blast: it proved to

right *Delta's first win at Thirlestane, with Bill King of Pedigree Chum (left) and syndicate members Barbara Thomson and Ian Mackenzie (right)*

be a good decision. I remember everything was going well until we were stopped on the cross-country – and the next fence was the most enormous footbridge. I recall walking around with Natasha Wheeler, who had also been stopped, and said to each other: 'What on earth are we going to do?' This was one hell of a fence, and certainly not one you wanted to tackle in cold blood. When we were restarted Natasha took the long option, but I was in a position to win, so I thought 'What the hell!' and picked Delta up – and she just flew it as if it was a Pony Club fence. We were the only combination to finish inside the optimum time, and collected the Scottish championship title. This was a lovely note on which Delta could leave Britain.

'We were the only combination to finish inside the optimum time, and collected the Scottish championship title.'

She went home with Messiah, and is now the mother of two foals, Mossie and Squito: Mossie looks just like her mother and is by Argonaut Style, a good racing sire. She is just as bad a timewaster as her mother, and will only be caught with a bucket of feed. Squito is by Prince Ferdinand, an English Thoroughbred sire imported into New Zealand; he is leggier and bigger and looks the part already. If he has half his mother's jumping ability, he'll be a great event horse – but I'll be retired by the time he's ready so perhaps he'll give Jo a second chance.

below *Delta with her first baby, a filly – Mossie – by Argonaut Style*

4 the kiwi belles' ASPYRING

'Aspyring has proved a wonderful successor to Messiah and Ricochet, and he has been a prolific winner for some of my strongest supporters, the Kiwi Belles Syndicate.'

Aspyring has proved a wonderful successor to Messiah and Ricochet, and he has been a prolific winner for some of my strongest supporters, the Kiwi Belles Syndicate. But rather like Ricochet, Aspyring – known as 'Boz' at home – was always destined to be an understudy, due this time to the brilliance of Chesterfield and Ready Teddy.

Boz was produced in New Zealand to intermediate level by a friend of mine, Janine Hayde, and she was always telling me at the time what a lovely horse she had. He actually lived on my property in New Zealand, as Janine was renting it from me, but I hadn't seen him compete. She was good enough to show him to me before any other buyers, and after trying him I decided to sell a novice horse owned by the Kiwi Belles, and purchase him.

'We all get together every Christmas to talk about the horses' programmes, and they've become great friends.'

The Kiwi Belles Syndicate was initiated by Heather MacRae, who owned Rata. After Stockholm when sponsorship was not forthcoming she started helping me with young horses, and persuaded some friends to join her: Margaret Trotter, Margs Apatu and Joyce Fisher, who is elderly and doesn't travel, but follows the horses with great interest and even gets up at 6am to listen to the world sports news. We all get together every Christmas to talk about the horses' programmes, and they've become great friends. I hope they've had a lot of fun, too. I was particularly pleased when Boz, along with

above The Kiwi Belles: Lady Margaret Trotter, Margs Apatu, Joyce Fisher and Heather MacRae

left An early run together in New Zealand, at Taupo

Toad Hall and Rangitoto, helped win them the Stibbe Owners' Cup at the PERA awards in the first year it was presented.

I bought Boz at Christmas in 1993, and brought him over by boat to the UK in March 1994 after riding him just once at home. He was immediately successful, and in 1994 won me two three-star three-day events, Bramham and Boekelo; I also took him to the World Games as understudy to Delta.

At first I found Boz very strong across country, but although he still pulls strongly, now he is more settled in his mind. He was the best horse I'd had on the flat at that stage – a Thoroughbred that could really move, and what is more, didn't hot up – and this was something of a novelty!

'He was immediately successful, and in 1994 won me two three-star three-day events, Bramham and Boekelo; I also took him to the World Games as understudy to Delta.'

right *En route to winning Bramham in 1994*

above *Victory lap at Bramham*

As a result he was a prolific winner of one-day events, and when we won Bramham and Boekelo it was having had a significant lead after the dressage on both occasions.

However, management was 90 per cent of the key to success with Boz, because although he has legs of steel he has shallow, flat feet and he was either out winning or he was limping. He would go lame that quickly – in The Hague he was suddenly lame at the initial trot-up – and he has always been susceptible to bruising and corns. He is now shod regularly, every four weeks at least; he has remedial shoeing; and he wears leather pads all the time to take the concussion out of the ground. But in spite of these problems, he still goes best on firm going.

I had high hopes of Boz in 1995, and obviously he was an Atlanta prospect – but then disaster struck. At Brigstock horse trials he faltered coming out of a water jump, and missed the sleepered bank out with his hindlegs. He didn't fall, however, just popped up like a kangaroo, and he carried on to be placed; but he had skinned his hock and afterwards he got progressively lamer behind. We assumed that the graze on the hock was the problem, but he didn't seem to be making any

'... a Thoroughbred that could really move, and what is more, didn't hot up – and this was something of a novelty!'

'... although Boz is a brave, genuine horse who doesn't have a mean bone in his body, he is also a serious worrier who always thinks he's doing something wrong.'

progress – and eventually it was discovered, to everyone's horror, that he had broken the pedal bone in one hind foot – it had split clean up the centre.

Bobby McEwen of the Ridgeway Veterinary Group, who does all my horses, inserted a screw to make the bone come together, as it had split like a peg. He still has the screw in there. Bobby did a great job, but he warned us that Boz would be lame for six months – and he also made it quite clear to us that in fact there was no guarantee that he would ever come right. But in exactly six months he came sound, and we've never given it a second thought. I was absolutely devastated at the time, but Boz has certainly made up for it since.

Another problem he has is an allergy which makes him sneeze constantly from mid-June to mid-August. He doesn't do it when you're riding him or when he is in the field, but dust particles in the stable are a nightmare for him. He stops immediately if you give him anti-histamine, but of course that is against the rules in a competition.

I started working him at Christmas time in 1995, and had high hopes of him for the Atlanta Olympics in 1996, as my other top horses were Chesterfield, who was new, and Ready Teddy, who was just a novice. As a result I rather rushed the spring preparation, and

below *At Badminton 1996, before our slip-up*

left Jumping into the Badminton lake

ASPYRING

BORN	1985
OWNER	Kiwi Belles Syndicate
BREEDING	NZ Thoroughbred by Ring The Bell out of Donna Estelle
COLOUR	Chestnut
HEIGHT	16.1hh

Career highlights

1994	1st Bramham, 1st Boekelo
1996	4th Boekelo
1997	1st Luhmühlen, 2nd Achselschwang
1998	9th Badminton, 2nd Burghley
1999	2nd Lexington

set off bravely – or foolishly – for Badminton. This was a big mistake, however, because although Boz is a brave, genuine horse who doesn't have a mean bone in his body, he is also a serious worrier who always thinks he's doing something wrong. You can never give him a severe reprimand, as even a change of voice worries him. If he can't work out the point of an exercise, he gets really fraught – he simply doesn't have an analytical mind. For this reason you mustn't test him too much in training, either, because basically if he can't work out how to please you, he will rather panic and just get faster and faster, and compound the problem.

To cut a long story short, we had a fall going into the

'... if he can't work out how to please you, he will rather panic and just get faster and faster, and compound the problem.'

coffin at this Badminton because I was trying to ride him like my other horses, insisting on a very collected approach – but this worried him, so he resisted the aids and got it wrong. We then hit the upright rails and skidded into the ditch with me tangled up in his legs. It was very disappointing, especially as the selectors then lost interest in him, only remembering this fall at

'I needed to qualify him for the Olympics to ensure a second string to my bow, so I decided to take him to the three-star competition at Pratoni del Vivaro, in Italy. There he finished 2nd to Ready Teddy with a nice clear round ...'

right *At Pratoni in 1996 where he had to play second fiddle to Ready Teddy*

Badminton, rather than his two three-star wins. By now I realised that he certainly had the talent, but hadn't had the preparation; furthermore since that time I have learned to be more relaxed with him.

But I still thought I needed to qualify him for the Olympics to ensure a second string to my

above *Wide grins all round at Pratoni!*

bow, so I decided to take him to the three-star competition at Pratoni del Vivaro, in Italy. There he finished 2nd to Ready Teddy with a nice clear round – but by this stage the selectors were much more interested in Ted the wonder horse!

I was aware by now that the Badminton incident had knocked Boz's confidence, that he needed more mileage and that I should capitalise on his strengths. He is not the most athletic horse, being deep bodied and heavy for a Thoroughbred, although he is easy to get fit. However, he doesn't look like the classic event horse, as he appears either pot-bellied or ribby.

'I was aware by now that the Badminton incident had knocked Boz's confidence, that he needed more mileage and that I should capitalise on his strengths.'

After Pratoni we had the most amazingly successful run,

above On the roads and tracks at Pratoni in 1996

as he was 4th at Boekelo in 1996, and the following year won at Luhmühlen comfortably and was a good 2nd to Mary King and King Solomon at Achselschwang. This is an amazing record at three-star level – three 1sts, a 2nd and a 4th from five starts – and something for which he hasn't had real recognition. Boz has won over 1,000 horse trials points, he has often been my leading horse of the season and he has undoubtedly contributed to some of my five wins in the FEI world rankings; but although he is always robust across country, showjumping has been the weak link.

'At home he trains well, and he jumps nicely when he is relaxed, but under pressure he has a natural tendency to go up a gear and then he doesn't have the technique to go clear.'

At home he trains well, and he jumps nicely when he is relaxed, but under pressure he has a natural tendency to go up

a gear and then he doesn't have the technique to go clear. But by the end of 1997 he was getting better and better at showjumping, and I had high hopes for Badminton in 1998.

Unfortunately we didn't get off to a great start, thanks to some peculiar dressage marking. We were drawn early on the first morning, and like a lot of horses going at that stage – including Lucy Thompson's Welton Romance, one of the best horses in the dressage arena then – he was slaughtered by the judges. By the following afternoon it seemed that there were two different competitions, because Ted's test, which was certainly no better, was ten marks ahead of Boz! However, I was delighted with Boz across country; we didn't

add anything else to our dressage score and finished 9th, which was the best of all the horses who had done the first day's dressage.

'He is possibly the fastest horse I have ever had, and it is a minor regret that I haven't had the chance to see what he could do in racing.'

In the autumn I took him to Burghley with Chesterfield, and it was seriously wet. I have never enjoyed steeplechasing Boz at the best of times because he is so strong; it always feels as though he might not stay together, and on this occasion it was a particularly unpleasant feeling and we nearly fell. It was all but impossible to make the time because the ground was so deep; it felt as if we were going up and down on the spot. But Boz never gets tired; he is by Ring The Bell, who also sired the 1997 Grand National winner Lord Ghyllene, and he has a very clean wind. He is possibly the fastest horse I have ever had, and it is a minor regret that I haven't had the chance to see what he could do in racing.

Arriving at the D-box I discovered I was still in the lead on Chesterfield, and after my near miss with Boz on phase B, my enthusiasm for going across country at the end of the day in the pelting rain was waning, to say the least. But from the cosy safety of the ground, Paul and Fiona Fraser – Fiona was my groom – said cheerfully: 'No, no, don't worry; you'll be all right. Anyway, you can always pull up if you make a mistake!' So reluctantly I got on Boz in the belting rain – though because there were so many falls and hold-ups, I soon had to get off him again. To do this when you are just psyched up to go across country is an awful feeling.

Eventually we set off, and he jumped the first six fences really well – in fact I had a perfect ride until we got to the Trout Hatchery; here we rather scrambled through, but survived, and having got that far I thought I'd carry on. We jumped Capability's Cutting and the Dairy Mound well, so I thought 'Well, I'm half way round, I might as well keep going!' The only other fence still to come that really worried me was one called the Podiums, a double bounce of three rounded obstacles; I had nearly fallen off Chesterfield here, and I knew that if I couldn't

opposite top *On winning form at Luhmühlen in 1997*

opposite below *Aspyring trains well at home but doesn't cope well with pressure*

below *Final trot-up at Burghley, where he was 2nd to Chesterfield*

'... in fact I had a perfect ride until we got to the Trout Hatchery; here we rather scrambled through, but survived, and having got that far I thought I'd carry on.'

hold Boz we'd be in trouble. So I strangled him back to a virtual halt – in fact so much so that I thought I'd be penalised for stopping – but bless him, he clambered over each element as if they were Irish banks, and even shuffled in a stride between them. I was cross with myself for so nearly spoiling things for him, and from there on became determined to finish, for his sake. It had actually stopped raining, but the ground was sodden, with pools of water lying all over the end of the course. We had masses of time faults – but amazingly, we were still in 2nd place, and that is where we stayed.

At Burghley that year the FEI introduced a special 'grand slam' prize: US$250,000 to any rider who could win three four-star events consecutively. As the winner of Burghley (on Chesterfield) I obviously had to be the first rider to have a go, so in the spring of 1999 I set off with Aspyring for Kentucky to the new four-star competition there. It was a fun trip, but expensive, and I was grateful to the New Zealand Sports Foundation who underwrote our

below Dressage at Burghley 1998

left *Flying the Cottesmore Leap at a very wet Burghley in 1998*

below *Jumping under the Lion Bridge which, thank goodness, meant we were nearly home*

above An interesting trip to Lexington in the States, where we were 2nd

travelling costs, which were £7,500, as opposed to £30 for nipping down the road to Badminton! Kentucky is probably America's horsiest state and the setting is beautiful, with lovely old oak trees and miles and miles of rolling 'blue' grass. It is custom-built, unlike traditional venues in England such as Badminton and Burghley, and the facilities for the horses are superb, with wonderful stabling and sand arenas.

We got off to a slightly shaky start in the dressage, with Boz fluffing both flying changes, having been a bit bold in the medium canter; he dived onto his forehand and was late behind, so quite rightly we were marked down for those. The rest of the test was excellent, though, and we were placed 3rd. We then had our usual less-than-relaxed steeplechase round, made worse by the fact that there was a mix-up with my start time, and I was sent off in close proximity to a horse already on the course, which convinced Boz that he was making his racing debut! The fences were very small and it felt alarmingly like hurdling.

The cross-country was big and impressive to walk and caused quite a bit of trouble, but course builder Mike Etherington-Smith had done a good job, taking the sting out of the more serious technical fences by designing them with inviting rounded profiles in deference to what would have been a less experienced field than at a British four-star. My biggest concern was an upright rails and bounce into the water, and as Mark Todd and Stunning fell there just before I set off,

'... there was a mix-up with my start time and I was sent off in close proximity to a horse already on the course, which convinced Boz that he was making his racing debut!'

I decided not to risk it and took the long way, to keep Boz confident; however, even with wasting precious seconds here, we finished smack on the optimum time. Next day we showjumped clear, but our blip in the dressage meant our final score was only good enough for 2nd place behind Karen O'Connor; so that was the end of our quarter of a million dollars! I try not to dwell on the fact that under the usual scoring system I would have won – in 1999, international events were judged under a new, experimental scoring system – but at Badminton two weeks later, when I took Chesterfield and Ready Teddy, the whole thing went down the drain anyway.

Because I broke my leg at Burghley later on, Boz didn't get another run in 1999. He very much deserves to get his chance in 2000, for on both the occasions that he has finished second at a four-star he would have been a worthy winner; but with Chesterfield and Ready Teddy as stablemates he may be destined always to be waiting in the wings. Whatever happens, he will be retired after Sydney; at the moment I am trying to persuade Janine Hayde, now a mother of two, to have him back to do some leisurely dressage.

'Next day we showjumped clear, but our blip in the dressage meant our final score was only good enough for 2nd place behind Karen O'Connor; so that was the end of our quarter of a million dollars!'

left *Aspyring deserves his chance in 2000 – he has always suffered from being an understudy*

5 burghley champion CHESTERFIELD

I first noticed Chesterfield when he was being ridden by Melissa Bradley in the dressage phase of the Pukehohe three-day event and thought what a lovely horse he was, with a most expressive canter and lots of scope. Melissa had bought him as a three-year-old and brought him on by herself, doing an outstanding job. Then when I was out at the World Games in The Hague I heard the tragic news that Melissa had been killed in a car crash at home. She was only 23 and had just won a national scholarship for a leading young rider award. Her parents, Sue and Ewen Haglund, said that Melissa had once indicated that if she couldn't ride Chesterfield herself, then she would like either me or Mark Todd to realise his true potential. We were both invited to look at him, but Mark felt at that time he couldn't accommodate him. Melissa's parents were comfortable with me having the ride, and while I didn't think Chess had immediate championship potential, I did like him. He didn't blow you away with star

'Melissa had bought him as a three-year-old and brought him on by herself, doing an outstanding job.'

potential as some flashy young horses do, yet then turn out to be nothing, but right from the start I felt that I would be able to work with him. I can usually tell straightaway whether I will be able to work with a horse, and Chesterfield gave me an immediate feeling of confidence.

He is a very gentlemanly horse, free-going, amiable and totally uncomplicated. He also hates the cold and has a very bushy mane and tail – rather like a Thelwell pony – and he is the worst horse I have ever had to plait!

I had him flown over to the UK at the start of 1995, and pottered about with him at spring one-day events, getting him going at advanced level, which he hadn't done before. I took him to Bramham, where he finished 7th, and on the strength of this we were invited to join the New Zealand team for the Open European Championships at Pratoni. I hadn't meant to propel Chesterfield into the limelight so quickly, but I didn't

left and below *Chesterfield with the late Melissa Bradley, who produced him*

right *Exercising at our first Badminton*

have anything else to ride; besides, it was only supposed to be a three-star event, and as Kiwis, we weren't eligible for the European medals, so it didn't seem to be a competition of any great consequence to us. In fact we were quite a novice team, apart from Vicky Latta with Chief, as Mark rode Kayem, who hadn't done a great deal, and Andrew rode Two-Timer who had only done a two-star event. However, the competition was much stronger than we expected and the 'B team' went very well; I was 7th and the team finished 2nd, although technically we didn't get a proper medal.

Chess was 5th at Badminton in 1996, finishing on his dressage score, which was an amazing result considering he had only been advanced for a year. It was also to his credit that

'He is a very gentlemanly horse, free-going, amiable and totally uncomplicated ... he has a very bushy mane and tail – rather like a Thelwell pony – and he is the worst horse I have ever had to plait!'

opposite top *On our way to 5th place at Badminton in 1996*

opposite below *Warming up for dressage in Atlanta against a backdrop of misting fans and cooling shelters*

right *Chesterfield as team trailblazer in Atlanta*

we took the direct route through the Lake that year, where you had to jump into it through a boathouse. There were quite a few falls there, and later riders worked out that you could do the slow route and still finish within the time, but as we were near the start of the day we didn't know any better.

I was hopeful that Chess might be able to run in the individual competition at the Atlanta Olympics. However, in the end Kayem went lame just before the competition started and so we were needed for the team, as it was felt that in those circumstances Ted wasn't strong enough and I quite understood that.

The run-up to Atlanta was surrounded by hype because of the unsuitability of South Georgia in July as a site for a three-day event, and an enormous amount of research and debate took place as to how best to cater for the horses in such high humidity. In the end, thanks to the research, it was a huge success and a safe Games, which showed off our sport in a good light. But I must admit that I had my doubts when I found myself setting off on the roads and tracks at 6.15am! All this talk about humidity, and I was absolutely freezing! I was first to go, and because this climate was such an unknown

'I was first to go so I erred very much on the side of safety and didn't blast off in my normal way; I had the responsibility of being in a team ...'

quantity, I erred very much on the side of safety and didn't blast off in my normal way; I had the responsibility of being in a team, and felt concerned that I must get round. However, it didn't take long to realise that Chess was absolutely fine – by which time I had also discovered that, due to the early morning dew and also the large amount of watering that had been done, the ground was extremely slippery. It felt very unsafe, especially as there were some strange cambers on the track, and we very nearly came down in the same place that Australia's Gill Rolton slipped and broke her collarbone.

For the first time there was no individual glory to be had in this competition – the new format which was established in that Olympic year divided the team and individual competitions – so this was all about a team result. I knew if I had a fall that it would demoralise the others, so I played it safe and took one long route, at the Snake fence. We finished with about 20 time penalties, which seemed very disappointing until it turned out to be one of the fastest times of the day.

I immediately rang Sue Haglund in New Zealand to say that Chess had been a real star and that she should be proud of him. Of course she was in floods of tears, because every time Chess does well it just brings back memories of Melissa. The Haglunds

above In Atlanta's humid conditions both man and horse took advantage of the cooling fans

right On the 'chase at 6am – far too early!

opposite Launching into the main water complex in Atlanta

'We finished with about 20 time penalties, which seemed very disappointing until it turned out to be one of the fastest times of the day.'

have been the nicest possible owners; they have twice spent a lot of money on travelling across the world to Badminton only to see him not run, but they have never complained.

It was amazing that we eventually won the bronze medal because everything seemed to go wrong for the New Zealand team that day. Andrew had a stop on Jagermeister, who didn't take kindly to all the extra breather stops and got really tense and wound up, while Vicky had a frightening fall off Broadcast News at a bounce and couldn't continue because the horse had banged his nose. Vaughn's horse Bounce was due to go in the hottest part of the day and he was hating it – he was way below par, and Vaughn's sympathetic nursing of him to get him home was probably the riding performance of the day.

opposite Chesterfield showjumps clear on our way to team bronze

below Teddy and Chesterfield trot up in Atlanta

So it was a great team result, really. One of the best things about riding for New Zealand is that we only come together as a team at the competition; we don't subscribe to months of political team-building stuff beforehand because our federation considers us to be the most experienced members of our country in this sport and they just let us get on with our training separately. This means there is no dictatorship, no psycho-babble and no hype; we are all different personalities, but we get on well as a team: we rely heavily on each other for support, and we always stay upbeat, and all these traits were very evident in Atlanta.

Badminton 1997 was initially surrounded by controversy. There was an enormous entry and waiting list – qualifications have since been tightened – and so the decision was taken to limit foreign riders to one ride, while some British riders were allowed two. There was quite an uproar about this, with journalists asking people such as myself what I thought – and this is how my infamous 'Samantha Clippety-Clop' quote came about. My feeling was that Badminton couldn't be marketed as the best event in the world if spectators were going to be paying to see riders they'd never heard of – Samantha Clippety-Clop! – at the expense of leading riders and horses. After all, Wimbledon doesn't turn away the top tennis players in order to let in a lot of lower-ranked British players. However, I did also say that Miss Clippety-Clop had a perfect right to be at Badminton if she had qualified, and that it was the system that was at fault – but needless to say, I was misquoted, and this made me sound extremely arrogant.

The upshot was that, along with all the other foreign riders, I could take only one horse, Chesterfield, and I must admit that I was very nervous as I thought it would probably serve me right

573
N.Z.

C

if I fell off. But Chess acquitted himself really well and finished fourth on his dressage score.

We were hampered with our dressage mark because he doesn't have the best of trots – few Thoroughbreds really do – and he has a lot of knee action; but his canter is outstanding, very adjustable and up off the ground. The trouble is that in a test he trundles through the trot work and by the time you get to the canter the judges are not impressed. At that stage he simply couldn't execute the movements accurately and his lateral work was not great. But his best was yet to come, and he has become much more workmanlike. I always look forward to riding him in a competitive environment because it lifts him; he gets bored at home.

'... Badminton couldn't be marketed as the best event in the world if spectators were going to be paying to see riders they'd never heard of – Samantha Clippety-Clop! – at the expense of leading riders and horses.'

That autumn I dropped Chess back to three-star level for a bit of a break and took him to Boekelo, which he won in some style by 17 points. It was his first three-day win and he really deserved it, especially as he was the only horse to finish the cross-country inside the time.

We missed the Badminton of 1998 thanks to Ted kicking him on the forearm in the field, so he

opposite *Chess was my sole ride at Badminton 1997 – year of the infamous 'Samantha Clippety-Clop' quote!*

below left *Competing at Belton*

'I always look forward to riding him in a competitive environment because it lifts him; he gets bored at home.'

had a rest until the summer; and then he finished 4th at Gatcombe and won at Thirlestane Castle, giving me my fourth Scottish Open title. By this stage I had his dressage much more under control, and was quietly confident before Burghley.

I suppose I could always be accused of being a bit reactionary, and it didn't take long for me to make headlines at Burghley! The trouble is that you put so much time and effort into preparing for the big events that when something which is out of your control goes wrong, it is incredibly frustrating. I was first into the dressage arena, and while I didn't think that Chess had necessarily done a test which would have put him into the lead, it was workmanlike and accurate; so when I looked at our marks I was disappointed to discover that they showed a huge discrepancy between the judges. In fact it was more than a 10 per cent difference, which is a level the FEI itself says is unacceptable and must be examined by the judges. The second and third horses into the arena were also the victims of odd marking, and this is something the technical delegate should investigate, for it is not intended that the first riders in the draw should be treated as guinea pigs. Angela Tucker was the judge who had given me the lowest mark, and she offered the quite valid explanation that I had not shown enough lateral bend. I have to say here that if I was asked whom I would choose as a dressage judge, I would put Angela above most others, because as a rider herself, she has a great understanding of how a horse should go. Despite this incident, we are still great friends.

I was then invited to talk to the press about it all, and explained to them that Chess was my second string for the forthcoming World Games at Pratoni, and that if he was miles out of the running at the end of the two dressage days, I wouldn't risk running him across country at Burghley. Someone then asked me at what point I would withdraw, and I told them that it would be if I wasn't in the first fifteen. This, of course, made the headlines: 'Tait threatens to withdraw!' Fortunately Bill Henson, the director of Burghley, was delighted, as he got more coverage of the dressage days than ever before!

But on cross-country day it rained and rained,

below *Chesterfield gives me a fourth Scottish Open title, at Thirlestane 1998*

left Burghley 1998 – and that dressage mark

and it just shows how fortunes can change right around in this sport. Going first might have been a disadvantage in the dressage, but it meant that I got the best cross-country going. I tried to go as fast as I could safely go in the conditions, and apart from a very nasty moment where I was nearly unseated when Chess hit one of the Podium fences, a tight double bounce of huge rounded obstacles where we came in too strongly, we had a very good round and finished with twelve time faults. My overwhelming emotion was one of relief to have got home in one piece, and all I was anticipating was a placing, but we stayed in the lead all day as, thanks to the weather, the course caused absolute chaos.

We had a healthy lead, and next day, with Chess in the lead and Aspyring 2nd, it was all won bar the shouting, as long as I didn't fall off – and I didn't! The whole episode was reminiscent of Barcelona, another time when I had just wanted to give up as it seemed hopeless. As far as the weather was concerned, however, Burghley was a disaster, both for competitors and spectators, and this was sad because it is an event which has done a great deal for the sport in its efforts to provide good going and great facilities.

The next spring, 1999, I was convinced that I was going to win Badminton at last. Chesterfield had the best end of the draw (at the end) and he was really on song, with his flatwork the best it had ever been. Having been away in Kentucky just

'By this stage I had his dressage much more under control, and was quietly confident before Burghley.'

above Going first meant we had the best of the conditions at Burghley 1998

beforehand, I took him for a last-minute outing to Bicton to practise the dressage in a competitive atmosphere.

I had tied him up to the lorry, and I don't know what happened, whether it was another horse taking fright or going for him, but he pulled back sharply, which is something he never usually does. I didn't notice that he had any ill effects from this, so I cantered him next day on David Nicholson's racehorse gallops, where he was cruising and felt fine. However, he had gone off his food, which concerned us, and when he was turned out he didn't seem to want to put his head down. By the time he got to Badminton he definitely wasn't right, although he passed the trot-up. His neck was stiff and awkward instead of being soft and flexible, and Wally Neiderer, our team vet, and Mary Bromiley, the physio, both thought he probably had whiplash. Mary treated him, but he could only flex one way, and although by the Friday morning he was better, he was still not at his best; so I withdrew him, a decision which was most depressing for the Haglunds.

'But on cross-country day it rained and rained, and it just shows how fortunes can change ... Going first might have been a disadvantage in the dressage, but it meant that I got the best cross-country going.'

If any year was not to be Chesterfield's, it was 1999. I took him to the lovely new CIC at Chatsworth where we were in the lead before the cross-country. He was again going well when we came to the Ice Pond, a log suspended in water. He approached on the right stride and with his ears pricked – but then suddenly he seemed to disappear underneath me down the side of the log and banged his head. As a result he had to have stitches, and I felt awful because he was so bewildered. He just didn't understand what had happened to him, and he certainly didn't deserve it as his desire is always to please.

I then took him to Bramham where he was quite superb across country – it felt like a schooling run, with me just sitting there and steering – and we went into 2nd place. But again, it was not his day: he has always been a sound horse, but on this occasion he suddenly seemed unlevel behind and I thought he must have struck into himself. We gave him hot and cold poultices overnight, and although he wasn't himself, he was sound and passed the trot-up; and as we were in second place, it seemed worthwhile to continue. However, he brought two showjumps down with his back legs, which showed that he wasn't really right, and dropped to 3rd place. Obviously the placing wasn't the end of the world, but I felt sad for him.

I was hopeful of a good Burghley, however. Chesterfield always gives you confidence at a competition because you know that he's good in all three phases. Burghley 1999 definitely had a strong cross-country course, big and galloping. There were three waters in a row, which took their toll, and the third was a new Sunken Water where you jumped from light into dark, down into

CHESTERFIELD

BORN	1986
OWNER	The Haglund Partnership
BREEDING	NZ Thoroughbred by Haajii out of Waikore
COLOUR	Bay
HEIGHT	16.2hh

Career highlights

1995	7th Bramham, 7th Open European Championships
1996	5th Badminton, team bronze (and 3rd individually) Atlanta Olympics
1997	4th Badminton, 1st Boekelo
1998	1st Burghley, 1st Scottish Championships
1999	3rd Bramham

below A lap of honour after receiving the Burghley trophy from John Dale of Pedigree Chum and Lady Victoria Leatham, Burghley's hostess

water, up a bank and out over rails. It was a strong fence, but I wasn't worried about its design, and even now I am still not unhappy about it. But I made the mistake of watching too many other riders on the monitor where I saw one horse after another scramble through, putting in an extra stride on the bank and getting into difficulty. I made up my mind that I should keep the momentum going and not let Chess shuffle a stride.

We jumped the first nineteen fences to perfection and I was having the ride of my life – we were sixteen seconds up on the clock and might have gone into the lead – but I came into the Sunken Road too positively, too soon. If Chess has a weakness, it is to drift left through his shoulder; he would never run out, but he might go a little crooked. If I'd waited for just another half second Chess wouldn't have been confused, but as it was he went to the left, which was the shortest way across the water, became confused in the darkness, and attempting to bounce missed his hind legs on the bank out, and tripped. It felt as if we had been struck by a thunderbolt, and I shot out the front door and landed against the rails with my left leg still over his back. He stood up in a panic, and that's when my leg broke – in the same place it was broken thirteen years before.

I was left standing up holding my leg; the pain was excruciating and I nearly passed out. Strangely enough, the one emotion I felt was total acceptance: you never expect to hurt yourself, but I realised what had happened and there didn't seem to be any point in making a fuss. I do remember feeling self-conscious about holding up the competition, and wanting the medical team to move me out of the way as soon as possible. I also remember that the Spanish rider Enrique Sarasola was standing there, and he phoned back to Fi (Fiona Fraser, my groom) and to Paul, who

above *Taking the quick route out of the Gatcombe water*

opposite *Gatcombe 1999: en route to 3rd place in the British Open*

TIMBER WORLD

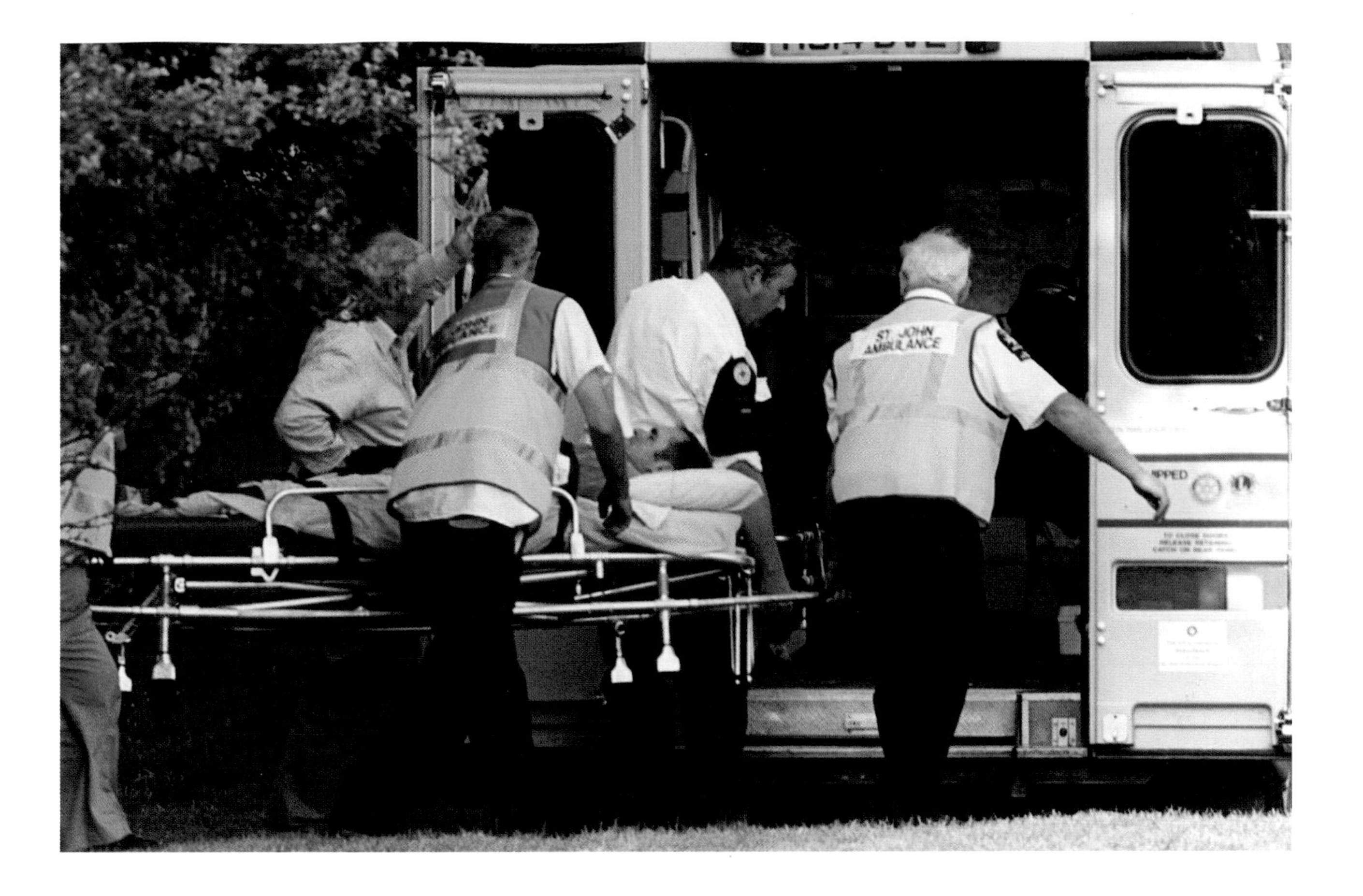

above Not quite what I had planned...

opposite Chesterfield jumps this huge corner in the arena at Burghley brilliantly, but minutes later we fell

were in the D-box: 'Don't worry, he's only broken his leg!' – which Fi interpreted as Chess having broken his leg, and was horrified!

I was also very lucky in the strength of the medical team on hand at Burghley, and just thanked my stars that I wasn't in some backwater when the accident happened. Remarkably, the orthopaedic surgeon who operated on me the following day, inserting a steel rod into my thigh, was actually there at the fence at the time. I ended up sharing an ambulance to the hospital in Peterborough with Panda Wilson, who had broken her collarbone. The worst of this experience was that when we got there, we learned that the awful news that Simon Long, who had fallen at the same fence earlier in the day, although in a different way to me, had died of his injuries. He was the fourth of five riders to die in 1999, and he died on the day after Polly Phillipps's funeral, which was a dreadful shock.

Chesterfield has been earmarked for Sydney, which will be his second Olympics, and after that he will be retired from major competitions. The plan has always been to retire him at the top and send him back to Sue and Ewen's property in New Zealand, where he will be competed at a lower level by Fiona, who will do her first advanced class on him. This should be a happy ending which is deserved all round; Chesterfield has been a wonderful horse to me, and Fiona, who is a capable rider, has dedicated five years to looking after him.

'I was left standing up holding my leg; the pain was excruciating and I nearly passed out ... I do remember feeling self-conscious about holding up the competition...'

'We did win our very first novice event, at Stilemans, but to predict that he would win Olympic and World titles would have been stretching credibility.'

and wasn't very sound when he arrived; in fact he hadn't travelled at all well, and really wasn't in very good shape at all when I got him in the autumn of 1994 as a six-year-old. There was no chance of competing him at that stage, so after a good rest I spent the winter working on him.

Right from the word go, Ted was an encouraging horse to train; I remember feeling excited about him, and was going round telling people that I'd got 'a rather nice horse at home'. In hindsight, this was quite an unusual state of affairs because many of the good four-star horses do not impress early on. We did win our very first novice event, at Stilemans, but to predict that he would win Olympic and World titles would have been stretching credibility. In fact I would have sold him at that stage as I had an Italian pupil called Caterina de Ferrari who was small and who would have suited him, but in the end she didn't have him and so Ted stayed with me.

__opposite right__ Ted is a victim of his own athleticism as he flounders in the water at Le Lion d'Angers

__below__ Ted was 11th at his first three-day at Blair Castle and I receive another watch for finishing nearest the optimum time!

Ted carried on winning regularly, and upgraded to advanced in one season. Our first three-day event was Blair Castle that summer, and I was thrilled with him. He was a bit green, but we finished 11th, and a couple of months later I took him to Le Lion d'Angers CCI**. He was fantastic across country there, where the course is no mean exercise for a baby horse, and we went into 7th place. However, there was a water complex where the direct route involved jumping off a bank onto the edge of the water, which was a flat landing. But Ted tried to jump down again into the water, and as it was a level surface, he landed hard and caught his elbow

with his stud, an injury which required stapling. This meant I couldn't showjump him on the final day – it was just one of those things, but it made me realise what an athletic horse I had.

In 1996 I had really planned just to consolidate his previous year, and was going to take him to the two-star CCI at Windsor. But plans changed dramatically when I needed to take Aspyring to Pratoni del Vivaro CCI*** to qualify him for the Olympics. Southern Italy was a long way to go with one horse, and as I wasn't expecting it to be a strong course and I knew there would be very few runners, I thought it would be a suitable quiet run for Ted, who had only done one advanced class. But when I got to Pratoni I was rather

'... and Ted just got better and better and jumped higher and higher. Next day he showjumped clear and won the competition: I realised that I had some horse!'

unnerved to find that the track hadn't been much reduced from the 1995 Open European Championships. However, there was nothing for it but to try, and Ted just got better and better and jumped higher and higher. Next day he showjumped clear and won the competition: I realised that I had some horse!

'Ted was seriously green in the dressage in Atlanta, but I was moved nearly to tears by how hard he tried and how well he went ...'

This win really attracted the selectors' attention, and suddenly Ted was a contender for the Olympic squad – as in fact any winner of a three-star competition would be when you're from a small eventing country. I was asked to take him to the Olympics as back-up to Chesterfield, which I agreed to as, realistically, I didn't think he'd get a run. But then Mark Todd and Kayem dropped out, and this left us a space in the individual competition: I suddenly realised the implications of this, and thought: 'Oh my God, now I'll have to put my money where my mouth is!'.

Ted was seriously green in the dressage in Atlanta, but I was moved nearly to tears by how hard he tried and how well he went; the combination of a Thoroughbred and a racehorse

above *He got better and better across country at Pratoni, which was his first three-star and a strong track*

right *Ted showjumps clear at Pratoni in 1996 to clinch his Olympic trip*

is never easy to start off in dressage, and he had only been doing it for eighteen months. We were lying midfield after the dressage and I knew we had a chance to improve our position: I had the advantage of having done the team competition already, so I knew that the course was jumpable and that the climatic conditions were safe. I also knew that other riders would be more conservative and that Ted was a quality Thoroughbred who could really gallop. And I was right, for by the time I set off, Sally Clark, who had started on the same dressage score as me, was way in the lead on Squirrel Hill.

I set out on the cross-country with the intention of going fast, as I knew Ted would tell me if he couldn't cope, and he just blasted off from start to finish. I suppose I was able to take advantage of his inexperience, as he'd never seen anything like this before and didn't know how to stop. He certainly proved to be more than equal to the task, although when we pulled up at the end he neighed and whinnied as if to say: 'I'm back – but what the hell was that out there?!' He never questions anything, but I realised that on this occasion the experience had left him a little shellshocked.

I had gone into the lead, but I couldn't get excited as it

was by no means certain that Ted would be able to run the next day. He had lost a shoe two-thirds of the way round and the hoof had broken back considerably and he had suffered a lot of bruising: it would be an all-night job to get him right. Our team blacksmith Alan Lambert and vet Wally Neiderer deserve gold medals of their own as, miraculously, Ted was sound next morning. He seemed to have grown inches, and trotted out really well.

above Fiona and our chef d'équipe Howard Hunter on their way to meet me after the steeplechase

opposite Trotting up Ted in Atlanta

below Fiona and Paul greet us after the dressage

I knew that Ted was a better showjumper than any other horse I'd had, and at that moment there was no other horse I would rather have been on; but on the down side he'd had a hard day the previous day – and Sally was breathing down my neck; I also knew she'd go clear on Squirrel Hill, which she did.

When I went into the showjumping arena I was feeling tense, to say the least, but Ted cleared the first fence by feet, and the next, and the next ... There were two spindly uprights near the end of the course and he did touch them behind, probably due to my lack of confidence, but somehow they stayed up. I kept looking behind me in disbelief, which caused Dad to ask afterwards: 'Did you think the Indians were coming?'.

Everyone rushed forward to congratulate me. It's hard to describe the euphoria of winning an Olympic gold medal.

'I knew that Ted was a better showjumper than any other horse I'd had, and at that moment there was no other horse I would rather have been on ...'

Atlanta 1996
575
575

NZ
Atlanta 1996
575
575

previous spread *Ted was more than equal to the task of the cross-country, showing characteristic exuberant jumping*

The overwhelming emotion at first was relief, but I really had to fight back the tears as I rode into the arena and everyone cheered, because at the same time I started thinking about how much Paul and Fiona had done at home, the efforts of Wally and Alan, and of course Dad – and I realised, perhaps for the first time, that this sport is far from a solo game. I realised, too, that I was in serious danger of choking, so after that I concentrated on complete trivia and stood on the podium grinning foolishly as the New Zealand National Anthem was played, because it was the only way to stop the tears.

Shortly after Atlanta I was flown home for celebrations in Whangarei. I was quite embarrassed and rather apprehensive, as I thought this could be a real non-event with only about three people turning out; but there was a crowd of about 15,000 to greet me, including schoolchildren waving banners! It was very humbling. The beauty of an Olympic gold medal as opposed to anything else in eventing is that it's something to which the

'The beauty of an Olympic gold medal as opposed to anything else in eventing is that it's something to which the whole world can relate.'

opposite *Nearly there – a tense showjumping round*

above *We did it!*

left *Showing off my gold medal to the press*

whole world can relate. Out of all my wins, it will easily be my most significant memory ever.

After Atlanta Ted began to mature. At first he had always wanted to play with the other horses in the field, and was very much the cheerful ruffian. By this time, however, he had grown from being the naughty child to the teacher, and now, no other horse is allowed to touch him. Yet he is still always in trouble, and whenever there's chaos in the yard, Ted is always at the bottom of it. One day he was particularly cross at having been left in his stable. Our horses live in an American-style barn, with a passageway running down in between the stabling. Ted's window was about four feet from the ground and it would only have been a few inches deeper than his girth, but somehow he managed to jump out and scamper off. Goodness knows how he did it, but he must have tucked his knees right up under his chin and jumped clean out from a standstill; there wasn't a mark on him, and as there would only have been an inch or two in leeway, it was an incredibly athletic feat. After that we covered up his window with a net to prevent a repeat escape!

It would have been easy to have let myself be carried away with Ted after Atlanta, but I managed to control myself and restricted him to a three-star the following spring, Punchestown, where he gave me another great ride and finished 6th. I spent the year trying to consolidate his work at advanced level and improve his dressage, for flying changes had been introduced into the four-star test, and this was a totally new movement to most event horses.

'I was having a fantastic ride: Ted had been immaculate through the Quarry and the Lake, we were two-thirds of the way round and I was perhaps feeling a bit complacent ...'

In the autumn we were selected for the team for the Open Europeans at Burghley where we finished 4th, on our dressage score; the team finished 2nd, again, to Great Britain. Therefore we went to his first Badminton, in 1998, with very high hopes.

At Badminton we had a favourable draw in the dressage, near the end, and Ted performed a good test, largely because he allowed himself to be ridden; up until that time it had all been a bit fragile. On cross-country day I was similarly full of confidence, as I had already gone clear on Aspyring. I was having a fantastic ride: Ted had been immaculate through the Quarry

opposite above *Party time in Atlanta*

opposite below *What a moment*

below *Consolidating a hectic 1996 with a successful run at Punchestown in 1997*

above *On our way to team silver and individual 4th place at the Burghley Open European in 1997*

and the Lake, we were two-thirds of the way round and I was perhaps feeling a bit complacent because I really wasn't having to work very hard. We flew over the Zig Zag and turned towards the Irish Bank – but here I just didn't ride him strongly enough; I didn't seem to be getting a good stride into it, and instead of kicking I just sat there waiting for the bank to come to me. Ted is a deliberate jumper and so he did a big jump up onto the bank, and was surprised to find a log on top; he shuffled a little stride in beforehand and as a result was too close to the log, and hit it. He didn't fall, but it was enough to unseat me. I was horrified, as I didn't think mistakes ever happened to me on this horse and I felt desperately dejected; but as he was all right I got back on and finished the course – which, of course, he jumped effortlessly.

'Although he is by no means the perfect dressage horse, this test was faultless and workmanlike and he certainly does have an arena presence.'

The rest of the year certainly picked up, however, and

top *Opening our spring 1998 account at Dynes Hall one-day event*

above *Pre-dressage at Badminton*

Ted and I won the British Open title at Gatcombe and the CIC at Scarvagh in Northern Ireland. Then at Burghley I was 1st and 2nd with Chesterfield and Aspyring, so it was a fantastic run – and yet I was pessimistically sure that the bubble would burst in Rome when we got to the World Games at Pratoni.

But this proved to be one of the easiest, most uneventful successes I have ever enjoyed. Everything went right. We were third to go for the team, so we had a quiet Friday morning

'At Badminton, in 1998, we had a favourable draw in the dressage, near the end, and Ted performed a good test, largely because he allowed himself to be ridden ...'

'The autumn of 1998 was so amazing that I was on the cover of *Eventing* a record three times in a row!'

SEPTEMBER 1998 £2.95

Eventing

THE INTERNATIONAL MAGAZINE FOR THE SP E TRIALS

9 770267 535041 09

TAIT & TEDDY triumph at GATCOMBE

Lucinda Green's cross-country MASTERCLASS

Sue Benson previews Burghley; Blenheim's Andy Griffiths speaks out; British team's new secret weapon revealed

right *With Paul and the two Fionas at the Rome World Games*

below *Chilling out at the WEG*

'... we had time to soak up the atmosphere and Ted could get used to the clapping. He doesn't mind gradual clapping, but if it goes from total silence to a roar of applause, he gets frightened.'

left Ted really excelled in the dressage at the WEG

draw in the dressage, which meant we had time to soak up the atmosphere and Ted could get used to the clapping. He doesn't mind gradual clapping, but if it goes from total silence to a roar of applause, he gets frightened. My critics would say that we were generously marked at this competition, but we did have the disadvantage of following a very fluent German horse. In fact Ted is really hard to fault when he is at his best, and on this occasion he was excellent. He has a big bend, a good half-pass, no irregularity in his stride and he can go in both directions with suppleness. Although he is by no means the perfect dressage horse, this test was faultless and workmanlike and he certainly does have an arena presence.

This performance was good enough to put us into 6th place, and the team into 2nd place behind Germany. Naturally I was filled with confidence, because the worst was over and I knew we had the best bits to come! When I walked the cross-country initially I did think it was straightforward, and that we'd be disadvantaged because others would be so

right and below *Hurray! The dressage is over!*

much better on the flat; but being 6th after dressage was an unexpected boost, and so I was really looking forward to the next day. I enjoy steeplechasing Ted more than any other horse because he jumps high but out of his stride and with plenty of pace, and he feels safe. I also knew that the roads and tracks at Pratoni were in good shape, and that in deference to the heavy overnight rain the cross-country course had had the sting taken out of it with the removal of two big downhill corners.

'He did look after me at one point ... there were two banks down to a narrow arrow-head, and as I was only riding him lightly he dropped back to a trot before the arrowhead. Other horses would have taken the opportunity to run out, but Ted is very honest and he definitely saved me there.'

Mark Todd was first to go for us with Broadcast News, and showed that you could achieve the optimum time without getting out of third gear; and, of course, Ted also found it easy and finished well within himself. He did look after me at one point, however: there were two banks down to a narrow arrowhead, and as I was only riding him lightly he dropped back to a trot before the arrowhead. Other horses would have taken the opportunity to run out, but Ted is very honest and he definitely saved me there.

Poor Sally Clark had a nightmare ride on Squirrel Hill, who didn't want to know and was

below Despite the conditions Ted found the WEG cross-country course easy

eliminated for five stops, but Vaughn was a great anchorman and brought Bounce home with just a few time penalties despite the deteriorating going. Although the course was perhaps on the soft side for a championship, I don't think it detracted from the competition at all, as many other nations were able to get their teams round, which was a good result.

The New Zealand team was way in the lead by this stage, and I was lying 4th behind Stuart Tinney, Bettina Overesch and Mark Todd. I realised that I might be in with a chance because I knew poor Bettina's horse Watermill Stream had lost a shoe and was sore – and in fact he did fail the trot-up – and Stuart's horse was an unknown quantity. However, I thought Broadcast News could

'I realised I might be in with a chance as poor Bettina's horse was sore and Stuart's was an unknown quantity ...'

above We finished easily inside the time

go clear for Mark, and he had a fence in hand anyway.

Overnight I started to convince myself that I was going to win. I was hell-bent on having a clear showjumping round, and Ted produced surely one of the best rounds that anyone will ever see from an event horse – and I did get that little bit of luck in that both Stuart and Mark had fences down. Even so, whatever my hopes had been, it was still with a sense of

below Ted produced one of the best rounds you'll ever see from an event horse

'I was hell-bent on having a clear showjumping round, and Ted produced surely one of the best rounds that anyone will ever see from an event horse ...'

sheer disbelief that I realised I had won my second world title. It was very hard on Mark though, as this was the one title that he'd been trying to win for exactly twenty years. Nevertheless it was the most fantastic result for New Zealand: not only did we win the team gold medal, but in the individual competition we finished 1st, 2nd, 4th (Vaughn) and 5th (Andrew Nicholson who was riding as an individual on New York), and it made Ted and me the first horse and rider ever to win both the world and Olympic titles.

On the other hand it seemed that Badminton wasn't destined to be a lucky event for Ted; and it also showed just how one's luck can change in this sport, because after all our success in 1998, the spring of 1999 proved to be a shaky build-up for us. We had our first run of the season at Little Gatcombe and were in the lead but, with only two cross-country fences left to go, I made a sharp turn on some rather choppy going and Ted slipped onto his side and landed on my knee, which resulted in extremely painful torn ligaments. Then at the new advanced event at

below left *Sheer disbelief – a second world title*

below right *Gold for New Zealand again: myself, Mark, Vaughn, Sally and our chef d'équipe Vicky Latta*

left *Competing in the inaugural Eventers' Grand Prix at Hickstead in 1998, where we were 3rd*

READY TEDDY

BORN	1988
OWNER	Bob and Glenise Tait
BREEDING	NZ TB by Brilliant Invader out of Double Summer
COLOUR	Chestnut
HEIGHT	16hh
STABLE NAME	Ted

Career highlights

1995	11th Blair Castle
1996	1st Pratoni del Vivaro, individual Olympic gold medal Atlanta
1997	6th Punchestown, 3rd British Open Championships, 4th Open European Championships
1998	1st British Open Championships, 1st Scarvagh, team and invidual gold Rome World Championships
1999	2nd Bonn-Rodderburg

Rolleston I made the mistake of running him in deep ground, which he hates, and he found himself slipping and sliding. In the water complex I had to throw him at the log out of the water and so he made a very rare mistake and breasted it; he just couldn't jump it and had to stop. The only good result was at Belton, where we finished 2nd. The best consolation was that on each occasion he had led the dressage, persuading me that we had really consolidated this phase.

Badminton 1999 didn't start very auspiciously either, as the clapping made Ted hot in the dressage and we ended up with a disappointing mark; but after that the competition completely fell to bits for us anyway. The weather was absolutely diabolical for cross-country day and we set off

'He is an ideal type for me: only 16hh, but so full of power and scope, and with a huge engine. I've been comfortable with him from the start, and I have to say that truly he's been a horse of a lifetime.'

reluctantly in the pouring rain; by this stage I think Ted was completely disheartened by British weather, and I didn't help by making a stupid decision at Tom Smith's Walls. I suddenly abandoned my intention of taking the long route, and decided to jump the direct route over the corner – but as I thought he was infallible I didn't show him exactly what I wanted, and rather threw him at it. Of course, he just ran past the fence at the last minute, but it wasn't his fault – to this day I don't think he knows that he ran out. I was so fed up with it all by this time that I just walked him home.

opposite *A horse of a lifetime*

below *Belton, our best spring run in 1999, where we were 2nd*

After that I realised that he hadn't been enjoying himself and that we needed to regroup and cheer him up. I took him to the three-star event at Bonn-Rodderburg in Germany for a confidence-boosting run on good ground where he wouldn't be punished for his extravagant jumping action. He did a great dressage test and whizzed around the cross-country to go into the lead. However, at this point we became another statistic as, for the first time ever, he had two showjumps down and we finished second to Andrew Hoy on Swizzle In. It had been hot on cross-country day and I suspected he'd slightly twisted his ankle, so I'd minimalised the showjumping warm-up. It was a restricted arena at Bonn-Rodderburg, with distractions like a band and lots of flags, so he became too fresh and aggressive and bumped out a couple of fences – which shows that even the best horses aren't machines. Even so, I was very pleased with the result.

By this stage Ted had done quite a mileage: ten three-day events in five years, which is a lot, and I decided not to run him in the autumn of 1999. As it happened I broke my leg at Burghley, so this turned out to be a good decision. He's full of cheek and character, and a break will have done him only good. He started so young, and is such a special horse that I am anxious to preserve him. You can't look into the future, but he will only be 16 when the 2004 Olympics take place and ... you never know. He is an ideal type for me: only 16hh, but so full of power, engine and scope. I've been comfortable with him from the start, and I have to say that truly he's been a horse of a lifetime.

Pedigree chum

chance RIDES

My first 'outside' ride was on Suzanne van Heyningen's Floating Light. I now rent a yard from Suzanne in Gloucestershire, and this was the start of my friendship with her; I won several classes with Floating Light and competed at Windsor. Nowadays, however, I have become much more cautious about taking chance rides. I once took a last-minute ride on Greg Watson's Ivor Chance and, despite falling off him on the first outing, was placed at Blenheim on him, which was fun. However, this isn't something I do regularly. Of course, I wouldn't turn down a really nice horse, but generally I have enough on my plate. There is too much at stake to risk getting injured on a chance ride and then being unable to ride my own horses at the major competitions.

opposite Delphy Dazzle at Burghley

Delphy Dazzle is probably the best known outside ride I have had. Clissy Bleekman [née Strachan] rode him for the British team in the Gawler World Championships, and by the time I got him he was, at sixteen, drawing towards the end of his career. He was a phenomenal horse with a considerable engine, but he was not the easiest to ride in dressage and showjumping. He was produced entirely by Clissy, and it took me some time to get to know him. We finished second at Luhmühlen in 1991 behind Pippa Funnell and Sir Barnaby, and at Burghley that year we were lying 10th after the cross-country – but then right at the end of the course I felt him take a couple of awkward strides, and sure enough, he pulled up lame. As Clissy naturally wanted to look after him and treat him immediately with medication, we had to withdraw him in accordance with FEI rules, as he obviously would not then have passed a dope test.

'Delphy Dazzle is probably the best known outside ride I have had ... He was a phenomenal horse with a considerable engine, but he was not the easiest to ride in dressage and showjumping.'

In the same year I rode Sandy Brookes's Shady Lane in the pre-Olympic event at Barcelona, and was third. The ride on him came from Bryce Newman, who had gone home to New Zealand, and it was through Bryce that I also got the ride on Tempo. Tempo was part Hanoverian and was one of the most quirky horses I have ridden. He taught me an awful lot because he would stop if he was placed too deep into a fence; he didn't have the technique to pick his knees up, so if I got him into a tight spot he would stop. For this reason I had some disappointments with Tempo; once we were well placed at Gatcombe but we 'missed' at the uphill fence after the folly and he ballooned to a stop. He was mostly genuine and a very useful second horse, but he couldn't take huge pressure.

In fact I had quite a few near-misses with Tempo. He was a great one-day-event horse, but he couldn't really stand up to a three-day. He won at Windsor for Bryce, and won the two-star CCI at Blair Castle for me, but he failed the trot-up at Burghley having been 4th after cross-country, and

01

he also failed at Badminton. He had an ankle problem and he was not good at trotting up at the best of times – although frustratingly, he was always fine on the Monday morning!

Tempo was eventually given to my vet Bobby McEwen and his wife Allie, and they had years of fun hunting and team-chasing him. He is now doing dressage and riding club competitions.

'In the same year I rode Sandy Brookes's Shady Lane in the pre-Olympic event at Barcelona, and was 3rd.'

The mare Just A Cracker – 'Popsie' – had probably the most natural talent of any horse I have ridden. She was a truly amazing jumper, and I used to have great fun in the indoor school

sticking the fences up higher and higher. She would just carry on ballooning over them and I would pretend to be a proper showjumper! She was also great on the flat, but at the same time she was a real handful and quite manic. She came out of the stable full of beans every day and often dumped pupils, and you had to ride her every inch of the way across country or she would duck out. When we arrived

'Tempo was part Hanoverian and was one of the most quirky horses I have ridden – he taught me an awful lot. If he was placed too deep into a fence he would stop.'

above *Shady Lane at the pre-Olympic event at Barcelona in 1991*

right *Tempo stretches over the corner in the water at Burghley 1995*

'The nature of an event rider's life means that you have to sell horses, however reluctantly, in order to afford to keep going; generally I try to buy and sell a young horse every year.'

at a competition, the first thing she would do was dig up her stable; at Boekelo one year she dug so hard that she actually brought up water and flooded the stable!

Popsie was bred by Penny Piggin; she was by Welton Crackerjack out of Gemma Jay, a good eventing mare who was 5th at Badminton with Sue Benson. The main problem with Just A Cracker was that she had upright pasterns which jarred badly, and this meant that she tended to get sore easily. She therefore missed quite a lot of preparation, and I always felt that it would not be fair to push her to the higher levels. However, we won the Chantilly two-star CCI and were 2nd at Boekelo (to Aspyring). Popsie could perhaps have showjumped successfully, as her mother did, but instead she became a brood mare. I enjoyed riding her hugely, as she jumped so correctly that you could always sit nicely on her – she definitely made the rider look good!

Ra Ora and By Jingo were two more good horses who came and went, as did Perhaps, who was longlisted for the British Young Rider team with Mark Tracey, and Boy Scout, who went to Italy. The nature of an event rider's life means that you have to sell horses, however reluctantly, in order to afford to keep going; generally I try to buy and sell a young horse every year.

At one stage I had three lovely grey horses: Rangitoto, Toad Hall and Eze, and I still have Eze. Rangitoto, who is named after a volcanic island in Auckland Harbour, and Eze, who was started off by Jo Shepherd, both came to me as complete novices; I found them in New Zealand as five-year-olds. Eze was bred by Bill Noble's mother-in-law Mary Glossop, and my buying him was a nice completion of a circle, as five years previously I had been to the sales with Mary to look at possible brood mares to breed dressage horses for Bill's wife Felicity – and Eze's dam was one of these.

right *Eze at Chantilly CIC in 1998*

Both horses upgraded quickly, and in fact I ran them at Le Lion d'Angers when they were six-year-olds; in hindsight this was rather a tough call, and something I wouldn't do again with southern hemisphere youngsters. The ownership of Eze was taken on by Ian Mackenzie, who was with me in New Zealand when I bought him. Eze hasn't really had the chance to shine yet; he won a lot to begin with, but then had some training setbacks and he missed 1999 due to, firstly, an old injury and then to my broken leg; but I hope to get him to three-star level. He is by Abalou, also the sire of Messiah and Delta, but he is quite different to those two, as although he is a good technician he is really rather lazy.

Rangitoto turned out to be too big for me. He was careful across country for a big horse and I enjoyed riding him, but I couldn't get the best out of him on the flat. Again, it was a case of the finances being more important, and when Ian Stark, who likes New Zealand horses, was looking for a horse for Lady Vestey, I had no hesitation in selling him. Ian liked him straightaway and he has gone well for Ian since, earning placings at three-star events; and it gives me a great feeling of pleasure to see them going well together.

'Eze hasn't really had the chance to shine yet; he won a lot to begin with, but then had some training setbacks ... due to, firstly, an old injury and then my broken leg ...'

Toad Hall, the third grey, was produced from off the racecourse by a New Zealand rider called Rachel Mackinnon, who had been successful with many other horses. However, she eventually became frustrated with him on the flat. I had always been keen on him, and eventually I persuaded her to part with him and the Kiwi Belles bought him for me. We won our first three-day event, at Waregem, and were placed at Saumur, Luhmühlen and Boekelo; he was also my reserve horse for the 1998 World Games. Toad Hall is a great cross-country

'Eze is by Abalou, also the sire of Messiah and Delta, but he is quite different to those two, as although he is a good technician he is really rather lazy.'

'Toad Hall won his first three-day event, at Waregem, and was placed at Saumur, Luhmühlen and Boekelo; he was also my reserve horse for the 1998 World Games.'

horse, but although he schooled well at home he could be a bit sharp on the flat at competitions. I knew the Italian rider Lara Villata was looking for a back-up horse for Sydney, and as she is of slight build and he is not a strong horse, I felt that he might suit her, as she would have more time to spend on him than I did. The first time she tried him she loved him, and I very much hope that she does make it to Sydney with him, as he is a lovely horse.

Currently I have three younger horses that I hope will have a future at top level. Haka is one, and I own him in partnership with Suzanne Van Heyningen and Ali Mead, a vet. I bought Haka as a four-year-old from Bryce Newman, who had got him off the track, and as Suzanne enjoys speculating with young horses, she was keen to take a share. She does all the preparation work, while I ride him at the competitions. He finished 4th at the two-star CCI at Punchestown in 1999, and is now advanced; he was due to be targeted at a three-star before my accident.

opposite *Welton Envoy at Ston Easton*

below *Toad Hall, a great cross-country horse*

I also have two six-year-olds: Cool Time (Fred), an ex-racehorse who was spotted by my father and bought cheaply, and Webster, another ex-racehorse who is owned by Cameron McRae.

Welton Envoy is my only non-New Zealand ride. He is owned by his breeders Sam and Linda Barr, and he was previously competed first by Leslie Law, who won Blarney three-day event with him as a six-year-old, and then by Charlotte Bathe. Sam and Linda like to be closely involved with their horses, and as Charlotte lives in Cambridgeshire, they decided to bring him closer to home and offered me the ride. He moves beautifully and has been very well produced, so he has won masses of one-day events.

Envoy is not a full Thoroughbred and is a bigger horse than I am used to, so I have had an interesting time learning how to manage him. For instance at Bramham in 1999 we were in the lead after the dressage, but he got away from me on the cross-country; I dropped my reins and lost him through the ropes, so we collected a significant number of time penalties and ended up in 5th place. I feel there is still a lot more to come from him, and he has certainly been very useful to me in that I have learnt a lot about flatwork.

For example, at first we struggled with the flying change as he had no concept of what I wanted, and as I was learning too, it was rather like the blind leading the blind. Eventually Pammy Hutton, who is used to riding the Welton horses, helped me. I sent Envoy to her and he came back absolutely push-button in the flying changes – which just shows that I still have plenty to learn!

future PLANS

At the moment I am still enjoying eventing as much as I ever have, but with me it is all or nothing and I am determined that when I do retire from the sport, it will be once and for all. I want to retire completely while I am still enjoying it and still successful, and not just peter out. The Athens Olympics in 2004 seems a long way off, but it is possible that I will get there; certainly I see myself continuing until the 2002 World Equestrian Games in Jerez, Spain, where I will be defending my title. I tend to be the sort of person who makes structured future plans, and Jerez is definitely a part of my next five-year plan.

'I want to retire completely while I am still enjoying it and still successful, and not just peter out.'

When I retire from competing I shall return to New Zealand where I would hope to get involved in some sporting projects. In the nearer future, however, I intend to do some more showjumping on a national level, and would like to have a horse for Grade A competitions. Recently I have also been involved with Toggi in developing a clothing range, and having never done anything else in my life except get up in the morning to ride horses, I would be very interested in more business involvement.

At the moment competition life does not give me the time to teach as much as I would like, and most of my clinics take place outside the competition season. I find teaching to be a good learning-process for myself, as you are having constantly to analyse and justify what you are telling your pupils. I also enjoy the challenge of communication that it brings, and find it rewarding.

Although I think – and hope! – that my riding has changed over the years, I have not changed in the type of horse I most like to ride. If anything, I am even more inclined towards the New Zealand Thoroughbred, as they are so tough and athletic, and such natural gallopers and jumpers. I like to have a natural, sympathetic relationship with a horse, rather than a horse that I can dominate. Nowadays I am fussier about how well they move, however, as standards in eventing have increased so much that it is now very difficult to win through ability in just two phases – the horse must excel in all three. Even so, his ability to gallop and jump is still my priority over dressage potential – over everything, in fact.

If I have learned anything over the years it is to appreciate and value my horses. When I first came to England I was totally competitive at the one-day events, but now I am much more conscious of the bigger picture, and I think I ride with more maturity at the one-days. All the horses I have had have tended to reach intermediate and advanced level fairly quickly, and I now realise the dangers of over-running them. Once I would always run across country come hell or high water; now if the going is too hard or too deep, or it is pouring with rain, I am much more inclined to put them back in the lorry and save them for another day.

Tinks Pottinger and Mark Todd were two of the first riders to show younger New Zealanders that it was possible to cross the world and achieve international success, and I like to think that Vicky Latta, Andrew Nicholson, Vaughn Jefferis and myself have continued to show the way. Our successes have definitely had an impact on the sport at home, which has developed tremendously; Puhinui is now one of the richest three-star three-day events in the world and receives a huge amount of sponsorship and media attention. It isn't possible for every aspiring New Zealand rider to come to England, and nowadays those that do so tend to have gained more experience at home than I did, but the culture is still very much that if you want to get noticed you've got to get to the bigger pond.

My own journey to England was definitely a gamble, but it certainly paid off. I would not have enjoyed anything like the success I've had if I had stayed at home and not taken the plunge.

A DAVID & CHARLES BOOK

Publisher: Pippa Rubinstein
Commissioning editor: Sue Viccars
Art editor: Sue Cleave
Designer: Diana Knapp
Production: Beverley Richardson

First published in the UK in 2000

A catalogue record for this book is available from the British Library.

ISBN 0 7153 0996 X

Printed in Hong Kong by Dai Nippon
for David & Charles
Brunel House Newton Abbot Devon